Something evil was approaching...

Jeremy stopped joking when he noticed something weird moving in the pond. Pointing to a spot in the water about 30 yards away, he asked, "Hey, what's that over there?"

Something about six feet long was skimming along the surface. "Whatever it is, it's heading straight toward us," said Kyle.

Before they could swim away from its path, the mysterious object closed in on them swiftly and silently. When they finally saw what it was, Jeremy gagged on a mouthful of water from shock while Kyle screamed in terror.

"Who is that?" shrieked Jeremy. "What is that?"

"It's Lars!" Kyle shouted before disappearing under the water.

TRUE GHOST STORIES

TOTALLY HAUNTED KIDS

Bruce Nash and Allan Zullo

Rainbow Bridge®
Troll Associates

Nash, Bruce M.
Totally haunted kids: true ghost stories / Bruce Nash and Allan Zullo.
p.   cm.
ISBN 0-8167-3538-7 (pbk.)
1. Ghost—Juvenile literature.   2. Ghost stories—Juvenile literature.
I. Zullo, Allan.   II. Title.
BF1461.N36   1995
133.1—dc20   94-18862

Cover photograph by Steve Dolce.
Special effects by Shi Chen.
Printed in the United States of America.
10 9 8 7 6 5 4 3 2 1

To Dave Bell, who, like the ghosts in this book,
always seems to know how to rise to the occasion.
— Bruce Nash

To Jayne Urschalitz, a vision of spirited friendship
and uncanny artistry.
— Allan Zullo

CONTENTS

DO YOU BELIEVE IN GHOSTS?

 **S**ome kids claim they have seen ghosts. Other kids say they've actually been haunted by them.

In many cases, experts were called in to investigate these so-called hauntings. Usually, the experts walked away baffled. All they knew for sure was that something weird had happened that could not fully be explained.

Totally Haunted Kids is a chilling collection of stories about spirits haunting everything from a playhouse to a funeral home. You'll read nine spine-tingling tales inspired, in part, on real-life cases taken from the files of noted ghost hunters. The names and places in the stories have been changed to protect everyone's privacy.

Do you believe in ghosts? You might after reading the spooky stories in this book!

THE FAMILY SECRET

aurice Monet puffed on his homemade pipe and leaned back in his rocking chair. He twirled one end of his graying waxed mustache and told his wife Marie, "I think the girls are old enough to hear about our family secret."

"Are you sure, Maurice?" she asked, putting down her knitting. "They're still so young and impressionable."

"Please, Grandpa!" pleaded Nicole Monet. "Tell us! We're old enough!"

"You've got to tell us now," added her sister Kim. "If you don't, we'll pull on your mustache and stuff your pipe with hay, and tickle you, and . . ."

"Oh, don't do that," laughed their grandfather. He cleared his throat and said in all seriousness, "Now, girls, this is going to sound real spooky, but it's not meant to scare you. It's meant to show you how strong love can be."

* * *

Nicole, 11, and Kim, 12, loved visiting their grandparents' cabin nestled in Missouri's Ozark Mountains, a few hours' drive from the girls' home in St. Louis. Every summer the sisters spent a month with their grandmother and grandfather, who encouraged them to enjoy the natural treasures of the countryside. The girls would tie their straight brown hair into ponytails and explore limestone caves, swim in bubbling springs, and fish in crystal-clear streams.

In the evening, the sisters would ask their grandparents questions about their family tree. The girls enjoyed hearing stories about their ancestors who came to America from France over a century ago to work in the area's lead mines.

On this hot summer night, with their grandparents relaxing in squeaky, hand-crafted rockers on the porch, the girls sat on the front railing and were all ears.

"We're waiting, Grandpa," said Nicole.

Deliberately prolonging the suspense, Maurice stuffed his pipe with a distinctive, sweet-smelling tobacco that he personally mixed from three different pouches. No other blend had quite the same aroma as Maurice's—a combination of fruity and pine scents. He sucked hard on his pipe. With gray smoke curling out of the side of his mouth, he began to reveal the eerie family secret.

"I'm going to tell you something that might give you the creeps," he announced. "We Monets have a history of communicating with loved ones . . ." he leaned forward and dropped his voice " . . . from beyond the grave." The girls' eyes grew wide in astonishment.

"It's true," he declared. "When a Monet dies, he or

she sometimes comes back as a ghost for just a brief moment, usually to offer comfort or give a message."

The girls glanced at each other and then giggled. "Grandpa, you're putting us on," said Nicole.

Maurice took a puff, squinted his eyes, and looked squarely at both kids. "May I be covered with molasses and tied to a stake over a hill of fire ants if I'm lying. My grandfather Pierre—your great-great-grandfather who worked in a lead mine near here over a hundred years ago—paid me a visit about a week after he died. I was only ten years old at the time and very sad that he had passed away.

"One night, I was sound asleep when my bed started bouncing up and down. I woke with a start—and saw a short, powerfully built man, his face streaked with grime. He was lifting and dropping my bed with one hand. I turned as white as my sheet, but then he smiled. I stared at him for the longest time before I realized that he was Grandpa Pierre—but as he looked when he was a young miner.

"Then he moved closer to me and I could feel his cold hand on my shoulder. He told me he was fine and that I should not shed any more tears for him. He wished me a long and healthy life and said I'd see him again when it was my turn to pass away. I took a deep breath to steady myself and closed my eyes for an instant. When I opened them, he had vanished.

"I shouted for my parents. They came charging into the room and I told them what happened. I thought it was a dream, but then my mama spotted footprints from lead dust on the floor at the foot of my bed. At the time, my daddy hadn't worked in the mines for weeks because he hurt his back. And I sure hadn't been near any mine.

"I knew then that my grandfather paid me a visit after his death to soothe my heart. What clinched it for me was a couple of days later when my cousin Bridgette told me about a ghostly visit from her father a few years earlier.

"Her father Marcel Monet—my uncle and your great-great-uncle—was a trapper who was away from home for days at a time. One night, he appeared to Bridgette in the family's cabin with blood on his clothes. She wanted to help him, but Marcel held up his hands and said, 'It's too late, I came to say good-bye.'

"Bridgette asked where he was going and Marcel replied, 'Far, far away and I won't be coming back. I'm counting on you to help your mother take care of your younger sisters.' Then he disappeared. Two days later, some hunters found Marcel's body in the woods. He had been shot to death. Don't know if it was an accident or murder. They figured he'd been dead for several days."

"Grandpa, you're giving me the chills," said Nicole.

"Do you want me to go on?" Maurice asked.

"There's more?" said Kim.

"Our family seems to have a gift," said Maurice. "We have such strong family ties that even upon our death, we have the power to reach out to the living at least one more time. Some Monet ghosts look like real flesh-and-blood people. Others are invisible but make their presence felt. Some talk. Some don't. Not every Monet who dies comes back as a ghost, but many do. One other thing, the ghosts usually appear only to children."

"Does that mean you'll visit us if you die?" asked Nicole.

"Perhaps I will. At least, I'll try very hard."

"I hope it's not for a long, long time," said Kim.

"Me too, sweetheart, me too."

* * *

A few days later, Nicole and Kim went on a day-long hike in the Ozark countryside. They put sandwiches and water in their backpacks and brought along a flashlight in case they found a new cave worth exploring.

During their trek, they spotted a family of red foxes that scurried into the brush. The girls, wanting to get a closer look, stepped off the path and began to search. Suddenly Kim heard a loud crack followed by a startled cry from Nicole. "Heeeelp!" Kim turned but couldn't find her sister. "Nicole! Nicole! Where are you?"

"Down here!"

Kim quickly spotted a hole in the ground about ten yards away. Some rotted wooden boards hidden by years of fallen leaves and wind-blown dirt had covered a vent to an old, abandoned lead mine. When Nicole unknowingly had walked on them, the decayed boards snapped, causing the girl to plunge about 12 feet straight down.

"Are you okay?" asked Kim.

"I think so," Nicole replied. "I sprained my ankle, but otherwise I'm not hurt."

"I'm going to try to get you out." Kim whipped off her backpack and emptied it. Getting on her stomach, she inched to the edge of the hole. Then she lowered the backpack while holding on to one end of it. "Grab the other end of the backpack and I'll try to pull you up."

Nicole jumped several times off her good foot, but couldn't reach the backpack. "It's no use. I'm not tall enough."

"Okay, we'll try something else." Kim searched the area until she found a long sturdy branch from a hickory tree and lowered it into the hole until Nicole clutched the other end. Then, with all her might, Kim, who prided herself on her strength, tried to pull Nicole up. While holding onto the stick, Nicole went into a sitting position, put her feet flat against the side of the shaft, and tried "walking" up. As she neared the top, the edge of the vent's hole gave way and both girls fell to the bottom with a sickening thud.

"Are you all right?" Nicole asked.

"My arm," moaned Kim. "It really hurts."

"This is just great," said Nicole, her voice tightening with anxiety. "I'm hopping on one good foot and you've got only one good arm."

"And we're stuck in a hole in the middle of nowhere, and no one knows we're here."

"What are we going to do?" asked Nicole.

Kim took a deep breath, hoping to calm herself so she could think clearly. "Get on my shoulders and maybe you can reach the top and pull yourself out." Nicole climbed on Kim's back and gripped the top edge of the opening with her fingers. But as soon as she started to pull herself up, the edge gave way, sending dirt raining down on the girls.

"This isn't going to work," said Kim. She thought a moment and then sighed. "It might be scary, but I think we need to go further into the mine to find another way out."

"What if we get lost?"

"We don't have any choice."

With their flashlight on and Kim in the lead, the two sisters carefully moved deeper into the dark shaft until they reached an intersecting tunnel.

"Which way should we go?" asked Kim. "Left? Right? Straight ahead?" She felt a hand, cold and shaky, on her right shoulder, gently nudging her to the left. Gee, Nicole's hand is like ice, thought Kim. Without looking around, she said, "Okay, we'll take the left one."

About ten minutes later, they stopped at another intersecting tunnel. "Now which way?" asked Nicole.

"You chose the direction the last time," answered Kim. "I'm just following your hunch."

"Huh? I didn't tell you which way to go."

Not really paying attention to what her sister had said, Kim suggested, "Let's go straight." But the same cold hand grabbed her right hand and gave a gentle yank. "Okay, Nicole, if that's what you want. We'll go to the right."

"I was just thinking we should go left," said Nicole.

"Then why did you give me a pull to the right?"

"I didn't touch you."

Kim gulped and instantly had a sickening sensation in her stomach. Her body twitched. "Twice I felt an icy cold hand. If it wasn't you, then whose was it?"

"I think this mine is playing games with you."

"Maybe you're right. It's probably just my imagination. But let's go to the right anyway." The girls had no idea where they were going; only that they were caught in a maze that, they feared, had no beginning and no end. After about an hour of walking, they felt totally lost—and afraid.

"I'm scared," confessed Nicole. "I'm fighting this terrible feeling that we'll never get out of here alive." Her voice cracking, she said, "We ate all our food at lunch, and all we've got left is water and one granola bar."

Wondering what to do next, Nicole leaned against a support beam. It groaned and dirt trickled from the ceiling. Suddenly, two hands pressed against her back and pushed her forward. A second later, the heavy piece of timber crashed down right where she had stood.

"Come on! Let's get out of here! The roof is caving in!" warned Kim. They scrambled farther into the mine as a section of the tunnel collapsed behind them. With the roar of the cave-in ringing in their ears, they ran into a large cavern where they stopped to catch their breath. Dust settling from the cave-in made breathing difficult, but at least they had survived.

"Well, there's no turning back now," Kim muttered.

"Thanks for pushing me out of the way of that falling beam," said Nicole.

"I didn't push you. I was in front of you, remember? I had the flashlight."

"What's going on here? First, you feel a hand on you and then I feel two hands on me. Now I'm really getting scared. You don't suppose that someone else is in here too, do you?" Nicole shuddered at the thought.

"Shhh. Do you hear something? Like a fluttering sound next to us?" Warily, Kim lifted the flashlight and pointed it behind her. Its beam fell upon a hideous creature—beady red eyes, pointed hairy ears, and a rat face baring tiny fangs. The girls screamed in terror and bolted to the other side of the cavern before Nicole tripped and fell, injuring her sprained ankle even more.

Shivering from pain, fear, and cold, Nicole curled up in a ball and wailed. "It was only a bat," said Kim. She aimed her flashlight toward the ceiling of the cavern and winced. She could see hundreds upon hundreds of bats hanging upside down with their wings draped around their bodies like miniature cloaked Draculas. Kim quickly turned off the flashlight before Nicole had a chance to see them.

"I can't go on much farther," said Nicole between sobs.

"Let's just take a rest," suggested Kim. The frightened girls held each other tightly and didn't say a word for about 15 minutes. Fighting the fear that no one would ever find them in the belly of the mine, Kim broke the silence. "We can't panic," she said sternly, as much to calm herself as her sister. "We can't just lay down and die. We have to keep moving."

"What about those invisible hands?"

"I don't know. Like you said earlier, maybe our minds are playing tricks on us. Maybe it's a ghost or something. But whatever it is, I think it's trying to help us. If we feel—or think we feel—a hand, let it guide us. What have we got to lose?"

"Nothing . . . except our lives."

Now the girls had a new worry. The batteries in their flashlight had worn down, and the beam began to fade. The sisters had to find a way out soon or they were doomed. When they reached another intersecting tunnel, the girls stood perfectly still and waited—out of fear and out of hope—to be touched by the hand.

Suddenly, Kim felt a gentle tug on the left sleeve of her shirt. "Is that you, Nicole?"

"No."

Kim swallowed hard. Her entire body tensed up and then she began to tremble. "I felt the hand—a tug to the left. And I didn't imagine it this time."

"I'm so scared, my teeth are chattering."

"Come on, let's go to the left."

Five minutes later, the flashlight gave out completely and the girls were thrown into pitch darkness. They could see nothing and hear only their own hearts beating wildly.

"What do you think it's like to die, Kim?"

"Don't talk like that," Kim snapped.

"If it has to be, I hope it comes quick." For Nicole, there was no sense being brave now. She had given up hope. All she wanted to do was lay down and wait to die.

"There has to be a way out of here," said Kim. "But where?"

"Hey, do you smell something?" asked Nicole.

Kim took a couple of deep breaths and smelled a trace of something familiar—something that had always made her feel cozy, happy, and secure. "It's like tobacco smoke."

"A sweet smell like, like —"

"Grandpa's pipe!"

"Are we imagining all this?" asked Nicole.

"No, I can definitely smell it. It's coming from ahead

of us. Let's go!" Carefully, the girls pressed themselves against the side of the mine shaft and felt their way inch by inch toward the scent. There was no doubt about it. That was their grandfather's special blend! They turned left at one tunnel, then right at another, following the aroma that grew stronger with each step. Soon, they felt a change in the air—an ever-so-slight whiff of a warm breeze. And the smell of the tobacco.

For the first time in hours, renewed hope surged through the girls. Sniffing constantly until they were dizzy, the sisters groped their way, hoping and praying that the scent would lead them to safety. The air kept feeling a little warmer and fresher until . . .

"I see light!" Kim shouted with glee. Many yards ahead, a slender line of faded light split the darkness and grew brighter the closer they got to it. Within 30 minutes, relief and happiness washed over the girls. They had reached another vent in the mine's ceiling, about half as high as the one they fell in. They hugged each other under the rays of the late afternoon sun.

The girls danced and cheered. Then they looked up and saw the most welcome face in the world grinning down at them.

"Grandpa! Grandpa!" they whooped joyously.

Puffing on his corncob pipe and tweaking his mustache, Maurice Monet smiled warmly at them. Without saying a word, he pointed to a big rock in the mine. The girls rolled it over to the opening and used it to climb out of what they once thought would be their tomb. When they were freed, they expected to jump into their grandfather's waiting arms. But he wasn't there.

"Where's Grandpa?" wondered Nicole, looking in all directions.

"I don't know," replied her bewildered sister. "He has to be here. I can still smell his tobacco smoke. Why wouldn't he wait for us?"

Two hours later, about 6 P.M., the exhausted but happy girls arrived back at their grandparents' cabin where several cars and pickups were parked out front. When Kim and Nicole walked inside, they immediately knew something was wrong. More than a dozen people, mostly neighbors from up the road, looked sad-faced and teary-eyed.

Grandma Marie rushed over to the sisters and smothered them with a big long embrace. "Where have you girls been? We've been worried sick about you."

"We stumbled into the shaft of an abandoned mine and couldn't get out," Kim explained. "We got lost in there and then our flashlight gave out."

"We thought for sure we were going to die," added Nicole. "But we found another opening. Then we saw Grandpa looking down from the shaft. But when we got out, he wasn't there. Where is he, Grandma?"

Grandma's lips began to quiver and her eyes welled with tears. "Girls," she said, desperately trying to get the words out, "your grandfather died about five hours ago. His heart gave out, probably from all that smoking and years of working in the mines."

"But that's impossible!" Kim argued. "We saw him not more than two hours ago!"

Grandma Marie shook her head. "Grandpa never left this house today until he died about one o'clock and they took him away."

Kim gasped, her mind trying to make sense of all this. Suddenly, it all became clear to her. "Grandma, when we were in the mine and didn't know which way to go, I felt a hand guide us. It had to be Grandpa's!"

"And I felt his hands push me out of the way of a falling beam," added Nicole.

"And we smelled his tobacco smoke and followed it to the opening. We wouldn't be here if it hadn't been for him."

Grandma sank in her chair and dabbed her eyes with her hanky. "He loved you both so very much," she said. "It was just like he said. The Monets have a way of communicating after they die. I guess your grandpa came back to save your lives."

THE FUNERAL HOME GHOST

**D**eon Thomas and Terrell Mercer didn't really want to spend an hour alone in an abandoned funeral home after midnight. But they knew that if they didn't, they'd be labeled cowards by their buddies.

It turned out to be the scariest night of their lives.

The two 12-year-olds lived in a neighborhood of modest houses and apartments near the downtown area, and they hung around with the older boys who were into sports. The kids stayed busy by playing basketball, stickball, and street football. If they did get into trouble, it was usually when they tried to prove how brave they were. They would hang trapeze-style from the fire escape of their apartment building or shinny up a telephone pole.

One night, after a spirited game of stickball played under the street lights, Deon, Terrell, and six older friends were sitting on the curb when the talk turned to the Anderson Funeral Home down the block. Built as a mansion decades ago, the two-story stone building had been empty for two years. Plywood scrawled with graffiti covered the basement and first-floor windows.

Shortly after the Anderson family went bankrupt and left town, the deserted funeral home got the reputation of being haunted. It began when a homeless man broke into the building one night and then fled in terror, babbling about a ghost. The neighbors reported seeing flickering lights through the second-story windows and hearing eerie banging sounds.

"My sister Kena says she has proof that a ghost roams the hallways," 15-year-old Trumaine Wilson told the group of youths as they cooled down after their stickball game.

"Your sister believes in fairies too," snapped Deon.

"Hey, man, I'm telling you the straight story. She and four other girls sneaked inside the place last week and held a seance. They sat around a candle and held hands hoping to talk to a spirit through Madam Rose. You know her. She's the old lady who wears a pink turban on her head and a bunch of beads around her neck.

"Anyway, Kena said it was spooky. They actually heard a ghost speak through Madam Rose. The ghost was named Cletis Price. He told them he wanted to rest in peace but he couldn't because he was trapped and forgotten. Nobody knew what he was talking about. Suddenly, doors started banging by themselves and the flame on the candle grew real big and then blew out. Everyone freaked. They ran out of there, screaming like mad."

"Listen to this," said Willy Smith, one of the older teens in the group. "I heard that some fraternity boys at the college broke into the place one night last month and got so scared they tore out of there."

"I don't believe in that stuff," Deon declared.

"Me either," added Terrell.

"You little guys talk big," Trumaine said. "But I bet you two couldn't spend an hour inside that funeral home at night without crying for your mamas."

Deon snapped back, "Bet you ten bucks we can."

Terrell grabbed Deon's arm and whispered, "Where are we going to get the money?" Deon waved him off with a confident flick of his wrist.

Trumaine turned to the others in the group and asked, "What do you say, guys? Want to pick up some money from Deon and Terrell?"

The other teens nodded.

"Easy money," declared Dominique.

"Can't lose," said Joey.

"Do we get to watch them cry?" asked B.J.

Staring at Terrell and sensing the youngster was ill at ease, Trumaine said, "You can't just stay in the first room you enter. You've got to visit all the rooms." He thought a moment and then added, "Okay, here's the deal. Next Saturday, during the day, I'll sneak into the funeral home and place a sheet of notebook paper with my signature on it in each room. The paper will be in plain view. Then at midnight, you two go in with a flashlight and collect all the sheets of paper to prove you went to each room. Once you've got them all, you can leave. We'll be guarding the entrance to make sure you don't chicken out."

"We won't chicken out," Deon declared. "Have the money ready when we come out with the sheets of paper."

"You're the ones who'd better have the ten bucks," said Trumaine, "or we might want to keep you inside that funeral home for a lot longer than you'd like."

* * *

Deon and Terrell sneaked out of their homes shortly before midnight and met Trumaine and the older boys in the alley behind the Anderson Funeral Home. Trumaine pried open a slab of plywood covering a broken basement window. He then stuck his hand inside and unlatched the window. "Okay, you two," he whispered. "This is the way in. Find the eight sheets of paper and stay inside for an hour, and the money is yours."

"No, tricks," warned Terrell. "Like sneaking in and trying to scare us."

"Hey, we're all here. Everyone but B.J.—and he went away for the weekend."

Trying their best to hide their nervousness, the two boys slipped through the window and dropped to the basement floor. Behind them, Trumaine slid the plywood back over the window. Then, in his best Dracula imitation, he shouted, "Watch out for those blood-sucking ghosts!"

The stale basement air reeked with mold, mildew, and traces of old chemicals. As Deon slowly waved their only flashlight, the boys could see a rusted tub, two stained porcelain tables, and an old floor-to-ceiling cabinet.

"I think this is where they worked on the stiffs," said Terrell. "They fixed up the dead bodies to make them look nice. Yuck!"

Suddenly, the boys heard a squeak, then some scratching, followed by another squeak.

"What's that?" asked Terrell, moving closer to his pal.

Deon aimed his flashlight toward the sound, wondering if they should get ready to flee—just in case. *There's no such things as ghosts, there's no such things as ghosts,* he repeated to himself. The beam caught something small, dark, and furry. Deon twitched at the sight and then let out a sigh of relief. "It's just a rat," he announced. "Hey, look! Here's one of Trumaine's papers right on the table. That's one."

Just then they heard the sound of chains rattling about ten feet away from them.

"Who's there?" asked Deon. The chains clattered again. Thinking—or, more accurately, hoping—it was one of the older boys, he shouted, "Okay, who is it? Joey? Dominique? Trumaine?"

The beam from the flashlight fell onto a chain-operated hoist, once used by the undertakers to bring the embalmed bodies from the preparation room to the viewing parlors upstairs.

"You go around one side of it and I'll go around the other," Deon whispered to Terrell. "We'll catch him." Cautiously, the boys crept to the other side of the hoist—but found no one there.

"Come on, let's go upstairs," said Terrell. "I don't like this room."

When they reached the top of the creaky steps, they opened the basement door and walked into the first-floor hallway. Seconds later . . . BAM! The door slammed shut behind them, startling the boys.

"A breeze?" asked Terrell.

"How? All the windows in the basement and first floor are boarded up," Deon replied.

With goose bumps crawling up their arms, they headed into a viewing parlor where a faint smell of incense lingered. They spotted a half-melted, unlit candle sitting in a wooden holder in the center of the room.

"This must be where they held that seance last week," said Deon. They walked past the candle as Deon shined his flashlight across the floor, looking for another sheet of paper. "There's one!" said Terrell. As he went to pick it up, the boys noticed their shadows flickering on the wall in front of them. They turned around and gasped.

The candle was burning a bright flame! Deon waved his flashlight from side to side but found no one else in the room. Terrell shivered. "This is either a pretty good trick or . . ." He didn't want to think about the "or" part.

Deon remained silent. He wanted to hide his true feelings—that he was having second thoughts about spending the midnight hour in a scary funeral home.

With enthusiasm for the bet lessening by the minute, the boys entered a second viewing parlor. After picking up another sheet of paper, Deon shouted, "Look, on the wall! What's that?"

A dark red liquid was oozing from the wall and dripping to the floor. Terrell grabbed the flashlight and stepped closer. "It's blood! Fresh blood!"

Before they could move, a crash echoed behind them. A glass globe from one of the light fixtures on the opposite wall had smashed to the floor. The glass wasn't the only thing that had shattered. So had the boys' nerves. They scrambled out into the hallway.

"Let's call this whole thing off and split," pleaded Terrell.

"I'd like to, but we can't," said Deon. "They'll laugh us right out of the neighborhood. I'm not real crazy about staying here. But if we leave now without getting the rest of those sheets of paper, they'll think we're wimps for sure. And we'll be out five bucks apiece."

Reluctantly, Terrell agreed to stick it out. They entered a third viewing parlor that was empty except for a pine casket resting on a couple of sawhorses.

"Do you suppose there's a body inside?" asked Terrell.

"I doubt it," replied Deon. "Maybe a skeleton . . . or maybe a vampire," he added with a grin.

"I dare you to go look," said Terrell.

"What's the matter? Are you scared?"

"No, well, maybe a little," Terrell admitted. "You go ahead first. You've got the flashlight. I'll be right behind you."

Deon warily walked up to the coffin. His hand slowly reached out toward the lid when . . . CREEEAAK! . . . The lid began to open by itself! Fear rooted the boys to the floor. Suddenly, the lid flung all the way open and a hideous-looking man dressed in a black cloak sprang upright and glowered at them. The flashlight caught a glimpse of the man's frightening face—wild eyes, jowly cheeks, a forehead lined with thick red scars, and a mean grimace that revealed a pair of yellow fangs.

The petrified boys screamed in terror. Deon dropped his flashlight, and, along with Terrell, scrambled toward the room's exit. But just as they reached the doorway, the door slammed shut in their faces.

"Open the door! Open the door!" Terrell cried out.

"I'm trying!" shouted Deon. "It's locked!" They both threw their shoulders against the door but it wouldn't budge.

By now, they could hear the footsteps of the monster coming closer and closer. The fear-crazed boys, screaming in terror, ran wildly and blindly around the room.

"You are dooooooomed," snarled the fiend.

Deon skidded to a stop. There was something familiar about that voice.

"You cannot escape the clutches of death," bellowed the monster.

Well, it's either him or me, Deon told himself. He listened for the cloaked figure to speak again and then ran straight toward the voice in the darkness. Deon plowed into the fiend and brought him down with a flying tackle. As he wrestled him on the floor, Deon yelled to Terrell, "I've got him! I've got him! Get the flashlight and help me!"

Terrell snatched the flashlight off the floor and ran toward Deon who grabbed the monster's face. It felt rubbery and loose—and then it came off in his hands! It was nothing more than a Halloween mask. Exposed underneath was B.J. Marshall, his 14-year-old cousin.

"B.J.! Why you . . ."

"Don't hit me!" said B.J. "I had to do it. I just had to do it!" Then he burst out laughing so hard that tears streamed down his face. Deon—furious and embarrassed, yet very much relieved—slugged B.J. in the ribs before getting off of him.

"You two were so funny," said B.J., trying to catch his breath from laughing so hard. "I really had you going, didn't I?"

"You did all this?" asked Terrell. "The chains in the basement?"

"I strung some wire to make them move."

"The basement door slamming shut by itself?"

"That was me."

"The blood on the wall?"

"Pig's blood," replied B.J. proudly. "I got it from the butcher down the street."

"And the candle?"

"What candle?"

"How did you light the candle in the first big room?"

"I don't know anything about a candle. I threw pig's blood on the wall and then I left."

"Who else is in here?"

"No one. Just me. I told everyone I'd be gone this weekend visiting my grandma. That way, no one would know what I was up to. I was afraid if anyone found out, they'd blow it and wouldn't keep it a secret from you. I wanted to scare you to death . . . and I did. You fell for it. I thought I'd bust a gut with all your crying and shouting."

"Very funny," Deon said sarcastically. "And we weren't crying."

"But you were screaming," said B.J. "Admit it, you were terrified that ghosts were going to get you."

"I don't believe in ghosts," Deon declared.

After listening to B.J., Terrell felt a sickening sensation in his stomach. "B.J., come clean. Did you light the candle in the other room?"

"Nope."

"Did you smash the glass light?"

"Nope."

"I've got another question," said Terrell. "How did you manage to have the door to this room close by itself and lock if you were in the coffin?"

"What are you talking about?" B.J. walked over to the door and tried to open it, but he couldn't. His huge smile disappeared. "Hey, I had nothing to do with this or the candle or the light breaking." He paused a moment and said, "Okay, I get it. This is payback time, right? You've locked the door and . . ."

Just then the door mysteriously swung wide open by itself. "Come on, let's get out of here!" shouted Terrell. They dashed into the hallway and headed for the basement door. But it was locked. "Try the other door!" They raced to the other end of the hall, but that door slammed shut before they could reach it.

"Let's go upstairs," said Deon. "Maybe we can break a window and go out on the roof." They ran up the steps, but at each turn, the doors slammed shut in front of them. Except one. When they opened it, the flashlight revealed it was only a closet.

"Now where?" moaned Deon. "The doors to all the rooms are locked and there are no windows in the hallway. We're trapped."

For a reason he could not explain, Terrell took the flashlight from Deon and aimed it back in the closet. On an otherwise empty shelf sat a squat container about the size of a teapot. He picked it up and set it on the floor. Taped to the top of the lid was the name Cletis Price. Terrell lifted the lid and looked inside. It was filled with gray ashes.

"Hey, that's a burial urn," said B.J. "Those are somebody's ashes."

"Yeah, Cletis Price's."

"Say," said B.J., "isn't that the ghost that Kena heard at the seance?"

Before Terrell could answer, they heard all the doors swing open at once. "Let's go!" shouted B.J.

"Wait," said Deon. "I'll be right back."

"Where are you going?" asked Terrell.

"I want to get Trumaine's papers. Otherwise we're out some dough." A minute later, he came back with a big smile. "I've got all of them. Now let's get out of here."

Terrell put the urn back on the shelf. But the moment he did, all the doors except the one to the closet slammed shut again. "Noooo! Not again!" Deon cried.

"Wait a second," said Terrell. He picked up the urn and walked out into the hallway. Incredibly, they could hear the doors opening again. "There's a connection between the urn and these doors . . ."

"We'll talk about it later," said Deon. "Let's get out of here—now!" He scampered down the steps followed by

B.J. and Terrell, who was carrying the urn. The hallway doors were wide open—and so was the once-locked basement door. The youths finally reached the preparation room and banged on the plywood that covered up the broken basement window. Moments later, Trumaine pushed the wood aside.

"Ten bucks, man!" Deon shouted gleefully as he shoved the sheets of paper in Trumaine's face. It was great to win the money, but it felt even better to leave the funeral parlor.

* * *

"I think I've figured it out," Terrell explained to Deon the next morning. "I talked to Kena about what Cletis Price's spirit told them at the seance. He said he wanted to rest in peace but he couldn't because he was trapped and forgotten. This urn was left forgotten in the empty funeral home. I think all he wanted was for someone to bury him in a cemetery. When we went inside the funeral home, he got our attention with the candle and the light breaking. The only way he could lead us to the urn was to close all the doors until we ended up in front of the closet."

"Now I get it," said Deon. "When you picked up the urn the doors opened. And then they closed when you first put it back."

A week later, the ashes of Cletis Price were buried in the city's public cemetery. And ever since, things have been quiet at the abandoned Anderson Funeral Home.

THE DESK OF EVIL

This would be perfect for your room," said Ryan Bradley's mother, eyeing an old oak desk in the back of an antique store. The solid grained wood gave the desk a stately, turn-of-the-century quality. It featured three drawers on the left side, one in the middle, and three on the right. "The desktop is big enough to hold your computer and still leave enough room for you to do your homework," Mrs. Bradley told her son. "What do you think?"

Ryan, 14, rubbed his hand over the top of the desk. Instantly, he felt chilled and his shoulders twitched. But he ignored the eerie sensation.

As he examined the desk further, Ryan could tell it had seen plenty of use, judging from the cigarette burns, nicks, and carved initials in the wood. But that's what gave it an old charm that appealed to Ryan. He and his whole family were history buffs. They lived in an antique-filled colonial-style house.

The owner of the antique shop, a short man with a big belly, approached the Bradleys. "We just received this desk two days ago from the estate of an old man who died recently," he explained. "The desk is in fine shape. I'm guessing it's at least 100 years old. Look at the fine craftsmanship—there's not a single nail in it, and all the pieces fit together with notches and grooves. It's mighty handsome." He opened the middle drawer and pulled out a black iron key. "Look at this. You can lock all the drawers. And the swivel chair goes with the desk."

Ryan sat in the wooden chair and spun around in the seat. "Hey, this is cool." But no sooner had the words come out when the chair's left arm broke off and landed on his foot. "Ouch!" he yelped. He was surprised by the amount of pain he felt, because the arm had fallen only about two feet.

"Oh, I'm terribly sorry," said the shop owner. "The arm must have been loose. I'll fix it immediately, and I'll knock 50 dollars off the price. I assure you, this desk is as solid as the oak tree it came from. And the chair is too."

"What do you say, Ryan?" asked his mother.

Ryan wasn't sure, but he needed a bigger desk in his room, and he could tell that his mother really wanted him to have it. So he uttered the words he would soon live to regret: "Let's buy it."

* * *

Ryan and his parents shoved the desk into the far corner of his bedroom, across from an oak chest of drawers and his antique pine bed. He set his computer, dictionary, and other reference books on the desk. Very organized for his age, Ryan put paper, spiral notebooks, and other small supplies in the left three drawers. In the middle drawer, he stuffed odds and ends like his Swiss army knife, extra pens, pencils and erasers, political buttons from the last school election, and souvenirs from past family trips. The right three drawers were reserved for his prized baseball cards—some in plastic sleeves, others neatly arranged in shoe boxes.

When he finished filling up the drawers, Ryan sat down in his chair, propped his feet up on the desk, and felt pleased with the new addition to his bedroom. *Not bad, not bad at all,* he told himself. *It fits right in with the rest of my furniture. I wonder who used to own it.*

If he had known, Ryan would have felt very uneasy.

That night, he locked the right-hand drawers—after all, they contained baseball cards that were worth several hundred dollars—and stuck the key in a small wood-carved box atop the nightstand by his bed.

Twice during the night, a knocking noise like a piece of wood banging against the hardwood floor stirred Ryan out of a sound sleep. When he opened his eyes both times, the noise stopped, making him wonder whether he was dreaming.

When Ryan woke up the next morning, he started to shuffle off to the bathroom when, out of the corner of his eye, he noticed that the right-hand drawers were wide open. He put on his glasses, looked inside the drawers, and saw that some of his baseball cards had been rearranged. Cards of Kansas City Royals and Chicago White Sox players were in the National League shoe box, while cards of Atlanta Braves and New York Mets players were stuffed in the American League box. Ryan hustled over to the nightstand and opened up the little wood box. The key was still inside.

I could have sworn I locked the drawers last night, he thought. *I'm positive I did. Robby must have gone through my cards.* He pounded on the bedroom door of his 13-year-old brother. "Robby! Get up!"

Robby sat up in bed and rubbed the sleep from his eyes. "What's your problem?"

"Were you snooping around in my desk, messing with my baseball cards?"

"No way," said Robby.

"My desk drawers were opened, and I had locked them last night."

"Well, it wasn't me," Robby snapped. "Now I've got a question for you. What was all that knocking coming from your room last night?"

"You heard it too? I don't know what it was. I thought I was dreaming it."

"And you *thought* you had locked your desk drawers. Now leave me alone." Robby plopped back on the pillow and threw the covers over his head.

That night, Ryan again locked the desk drawers, tested them to make sure they wouldn't open, and put the key under his pillow. Just as he was about to doze off, he heard a scratching noise coming from the desk. He flicked on the light, but everything seemed to be fine. He turned off the light and heard the noise again—like a knife carving wood. And then the room became deadly quiet.

Ryan fell fast asleep, unaware of the terror that awaited him.

The next morning, as he reached for his school books

on the desk, Ryan noticed his Swiss army knife lying next to the computer keyboard. What's this doing out? he wondered. It wasn't here last night when I did my homework. Ryan tried to open the middle drawer where the knife belonged, but it was still locked. Then he remembered the carving sound he had heard just before he dropped off to sleep.

Shoving aside papers and books, he carefully examined the top of the desk. For being 100 years old, the desk had its share of gouges, marks, and scratches. Nothing out of the ordinary except—*What's this?* Carved in the desktop were four strange jumbled "letters" each about an inch high:

EΛΙΓ

Ryan rubbed his fingers over the letters, which seemed quite fresh because they weren't worn or darkened by years of use. *I don't remember seeing those letters before. But maybe I hadn't noticed them. What do they mean? And why was my knife on the desk when I had locked it in the drawer?*

"Ryan! Hurry up or you'll miss the bus!" called his mother from downstairs.

"I'll be right down, Mom." He grabbed his books, but as he reached for a pen on the desk, he stopped. His mouth dropped open. Glancing at the smooth metal base of his desk lamp, Ryan could read the upside-down reflection of those carved letters. They spelled E V I L!

* * *

41

Throughout the day, Ryan tried to figure out who or what was behind the mysterious events. His chief suspect was still his brother. Robby had a motive—revenge. A week earlier at school, Ryan, as a practical joke, had switched the combination lock on Robby's locker so his brother couldn't open it. As a result, Robby had to spend a day in class without his books.

Maybe Robby sneaked into my room two nights ago, unlocked the drawers, and mixed up my cards, thought Ryan. *Then he banged on his side of the wall with a piece of wood to wake me up. The next day, he took my Swiss army knife out of the drawer before I locked up the desk. He slipped into my room at night and carved E V I L on the desktop. But why would he go through all that trouble? That's not his style. And if he didn't do it, then who did?*

When he returned home, Ryan cleared off the top of his desk and examined every square inch, looking for any other bizarre markings. He studied the desktop from all four sides. Near the center, he could make out a large J and an S scratched in the wood.

Ryan put his books, lamp, and computer back on the desktop and decided to forget about the last two nights. But what happened later that night was something he would never, ever forget for as long as he lived.

Because he had so much schoolwork, Ryan decided to stay home alone that night while his parents and brother went across town. His father, a respected judge, was giving a speech at a banquet, and they wouldn't be back until late. So Ryan microwaved a dinner that his mother had prepared for him and then trudged upstairs to his room to write a book report on his computer for English class.

While loading his compact disc player for background music, Ryan heard a BEEP . . . WHIRRR . . . BEEP, BEEP behind him. The computer had turned on—by itself! The screen then displayed the video game "Battle of the Space Zombies." Ryan stared in stunned amazement as several keys on the keyboard flicked up and down as if they had been pressed by unseen fingers. The keys aimed and fired the game's laser guns until all the space zombies were dead. Then two words flashed on and off the screen so fast that Ryan wasn't sure what they said, but he thought they read "YOU'RE NEXT!" Then the computer shut off by itself.

When he recovered from the shock, Ryan thought, *Marty. It has to be Marty!* Marty Bidwell was the brainiest computer nerd in school and also Ryan's best friend. *Man, that propeller head is good. This is his best stunt ever. He deserves a standing ovation.* Ryan reached for the phone on his desk and began dialing Marty's number. He heard several clicks in the receiver and then a scratchy voice hiss, "I will get you!"

"Hello! Hello! Marty is that you?" said Ryan. Nothing but static crackled on the other end. Ryan weakly put the phone back on the receiver and felt his blood run cold. Nervously drumming his fingers on top of the desk, Ryan wondered, *What's going on? What should I do?*

"Ow!" he cried. He felt a piercing pain in the little finger of his right hand. He screamed even louder when he discovered the cause of his pain. The stapler on the desk had slid over—by itself—and punched a staple into his finger! He tried to pry the stapler off. But like a hungry dog refusing to let go of a bone, the stapler remained firmly clamped on Ryan's finger.

As he struggled to free himself from the stapler's jaws, the middle desk drawer shot open and slammed into his stomach. It hit him with such force that it knocked the wind out of him and doubled him over. His face hit the top of the desk, causing his glasses to fall off and land by the keyboard.

Gasping for breath, holding his stomach, and bleeding from his finger, Ryan groped for his glasses. Just as he was about to reach them, they twisted into a knot by themselves and broke in half.

His mind jangled by fright, Ryan tried to understand all the horror swirling around him when his chair flipped backwards, sending him crashing to the floor. He scrambled to his feet, but then dove for cover when his dictionary flew off the desk and whizzed by him, only inches from his head. Then, one by one, all the other books on the desk hurled themselves at him. Ryan, still sprawled on the floor, rolled to his left and then to his right, dodging some books while getting whacked in the legs and back by others.

When the books were cleared from the desk, Ryan stood up, but then had to duck again to avoid getting stabbed by a new wave of weapons. Pens and sharpened pencils that he kept in a ceramic cup on the desk took aim at him. Like miniature arrows, they flew toward their terrified target. Flailing his arms, Ryan batted some of them down while others nailed him in the arm and chest. Pens that zipped past him stuck into the wall.

Is this a nightmare? Am I going crazy? In desperation, Ryan low-crawled toward the door. But the desk, taking on a shocking life of its own, began to thump, rumble, and shake. It vibrated faster and faster until the computer and desk lamp toppled and crashed. Then the desk screeched across the wood floor until it blocked the bedroom door.

There was only one other way out—to leap from the second-story window. Ryan bolted for the window and tried to yank it open. But it wouldn't budge. As Ryan banged on the window, the ceramic cup rocketed off the desk and clobbered him in the back of the head.

He slumped to the floor, and a strange silence filled the room. Wiping blood and sweat from his trembling hand, Ryan tried to figure out his options for survival. *Think, Ryan, think! If I'm going to get out of here alive, I've got to get past that desk. I need to muscle it out of the way in order to open the door.*

The desk, guarding the door like an armed soldier, stood still. Ryan took a deep breath and slowly advanced on the haunted piece of furniture. But when he got within five feet, the desk sprang to life and began thumping, its legs rising and falling a couple of inches off the floor. Then, without warning, the drawers opened and spewed out paper, folders, and baseball cards. With his arms cocked in front of his face, Ryan ran through the blizzard and grabbed one end of the desk and tried to push it out of the way. But the desk shoved back forcefully. Ryan would have been pinned to the wall if he hadn't jumped and slid stomach-first on the desk. Clutching both sides of the desktop, Ryan held on as the desk lifted off the floor and began to rock violently back and forth. Within seconds, the desk pitched him off like a bucking bronco tossing a rodeo rider.

As the dazed teenager started to pick himself up, he saw the desk tilt on its side for another assault. Ryan leaped out of the way a split second before the falling desk would have bashed him. He then hurdled over the desk and whipped open the door. He tore into the hallway, flew down the stairs, and dashed out of the house.

* * *

An hour later, Ryan's parents and brother found him sitting on the front step, shivering, with his arms wrapped around his knees and chin buried in his chest. Dried blood was on his arms and the back of his neck.

"Ryan!" his mother gasped. "What happened?"

"The desk," he mumbled without even looking at them. "It's evil . . . and it's alive."

"What are you talking about, son?" his father asked.

Ryan lifted his head, revealing cuts and bruises. "Dad, either I'm going completely crazy or I just fought with a possessed desk." Ryan then stunned his parents with a startling account of his battle with the desk. The Bradleys knew their son wouldn't lie to them, but his story seemed too incredible to believe. "Let's go take a look," said Judge Bradley.

"Don't go up there!" Ryan pleaded. "The desk will attack you!"

"Calm down, Ryan. I'm going upstairs and I'll be careful."

A few minutes later, Judge Bradley returned. "The room is a complete mess," he reported. "The computer and lamp are smashed, the floor has been gouged and scratched, books and paper are strewn everywhere, and pens are stuck in the wall."

"The desk, what about the desk?" asked Ryan.

"That's what's strange, son. You did say it was near the door and on its side when you jumped over it, right?" Ryan nodded. "Well, it was standing upright in the corner exactly where it's supposed to be. And so was the chair—although its arms are broken."

"Then the desk must have got up on its own and moved back to the corner," said Ryan. "Dad, we've got to get the desk and chair out of the house and destroy them before something else bad happens to us."

He gazed at his worried parents and his heart sank. "I can tell by the look on your faces that you don't believe me," he said sadly. Turning to his brother, he asked, "Robby, you believe me, don't you?"

Robby glanced away. "Well, I . . . um . . ."

"Ryan, we know something terrible has happened to you," said his mother. "Let's clean that blood off you first and get you calmed down. Then we'll talk."

Ryan reluctantly went inside, but he refused to go upstairs. While his parents sat on the couch on either side of Ryan and tried to comfort him, Robby went into his brother's bedroom to survey the damage. Robby felt scared, not because he believed Ryan's story—he didn't—but because he thought his brother was suffering from a serious mental problem.

He walked to the desk and leaned over it, studying the marks on its surface. His eyes locked onto the upside down EVIL carved in the wood. Then he heard a slight screech and felt a little nudge against his legs. *Did this desk just move?* he wondered. *Or am I catching what Ryan's got?*

The answer came quickly. The desk suddenly rose a

47

full six inches off the floor. Horrified, Robby began to backpedal. But before he could turn and run, the desk dropped to the floor, its left front leg slamming down hard on Robby's right foot. He let out a yowl and hobbled quickly out of the room.

From the top of the stairway, Robby hollered to his parents, "It's true! It's true! The desk is haunted!" The Bradleys left the house and spent a sleepless night in a hotel room.

The next morning, Judge Bradley announced that he was going to solve this mystery. The boys felt too shaken to attend school so they went with their father to the antique store to find out where the desk had come from.

"I was afraid if I told you, I would lose the sale," confessed the dealer. "You see, the desk came from the estate of Jeremiah Swope."

Judge Bradley let out a low whistle.

"Who's Jeremiah Swope?" asked Ryan.

"None other than the meanest man who ever lived in this town, maybe even the whole state," his father replied.

"The initials J.S. were carved on the desktop," said Ryan. "That must mean the desk was his."

"Kids, that could explain everything," said their dad. "Jeremiah Swope was a mean, cold-hearted miser his whole life. He had this thing about children—he hated them. Years ago, he bought apartment buildings and then threw out all the renters who had kids. He'd call the cops on any child who dared knock on his door, and he'd chase any neighborhood pet that wandered into his yard. At Halloween once, he put a big carved-up pumpkin out by the front door with a sign that said 'help yourself.' Kids reached in and screamed—there were live beetles inside."

"How do you know all this?" asked Robby.

"Because I was one of those kids," said his father.

"So how does that explain the attacking desk?" asked Ryan.

"About twenty years ago, some neighborhood kids saw Swope driving down the street. They yelled and made faces at him," Judge Bradley recalled. "Well, he shouted some awful things back, didn't watch where we was going, and smashed into a telephone pole. He was badly hurt and had to walk with a cane after that. So he tried to sue the kids. I was a young attorney at the time and managed to get the case thrown out of court. I'll never forget what he told me: 'I hate children so much that I'll haunt them even after I die.' After the injury, Swope spent most of his life working at that desk. Imagine how much hatred it has soaked up. That desk must be haunted by his evil spirit."

"What should we do with the desk?" asked Robby.

Judge Bradley threw his arms around his sons and said, "Boys, what do you say we go home and build a fire in the backyard. I know just the kind of wood to burn."

Back at the house, Judge Bradley told the boys, "The evil spirit hates only kids. It won't attack me. So I'll take the desk apart." Within a half hour, the drawers, desktop, chair, and other pieces were piled together in the backyard.

Judge Bradley picked up an axe and asked, "Who wants to take the first whack at turning this desk into splinters before we burn it?"

"I will," said Ryan. "With pleasure!"

THE
EERIE PRESENCE

**A**s long as she could remember, Heather Gooden had felt a presence in her bedroom. The 12-year-old couldn't really describe this feeling other than call it a sense that she wasn't alone.

One day, she decided to jot down her thoughts about this strange sensation in her diary. Stretched out stomach-first on her bed, Heather cocked her head to one side to keep her long blond hair from covering the page. Then, with a purple felt-tip pen, she wrote:

"Sometimes I think there's a ghost in my room. It's not an evil spirit. It's the ghost of someone nice. I haven't seen or heard anything strange, but I can feel this nice spirit touch me. Am I dreaming? I don't know.

"I just read what I wrote. It sounds *sooo* dumb! I must be the only girl in the whole world who thinks there's a nice ghost in her room. But I can't help it. I have this feeling, that's all."

Heather closed her diary, rolled over on her back, and gazed at the ceiling. She studied the swirls of plaster and the beautifully carved wood molding that trimmed the room in her 70-year-old house.

I wonder what people lived in this room, Heather thought. *Kids? Grown-ups? Did they like it here? Was this a happy room or a sad room? Did the spirit—if there really is one—use this room? Why do I think about this ghost only when I'm in this room?* Her mind drifted back, trying to recall the times when she thought the ghost had visited her.

Heather usually felt this presence whenever she was ill or very sad—which wasn't very often because she was a happy and healthy child. In her earliest recollection— she couldn't have been more than four years old— Heather was sick with a terrible cold. Her parents were out late that night at an important function, and her teenage sister Tracy was downstairs asleep on the couch with the TV on.

Heather, tossing and turning in bed, whimpered and had difficulty breathing because of a stuffy nose. Suddenly she felt someone pick her up, hold her gently, and rock her in a rocking chair. But then Heather realized that she herself was floating in the air inches above the moving rocker. She didn't cry or scream because she felt safe and warm.

Was it real or a dream?

Another time, when she was about seven years old, Heather suffered from a high fever. Her mother, also sick, was napping in the other bedroom. As Heather tried to doze off, she felt a hand gently stroking her forehead.

But when she opened her eyes, there was no one in the room.

Was the fever playing tricks on her?

About a year later, Heather had the strongest feeling yet of the presence. It happened on one of the worst days of her life. First, she got into a big fight with her best friend Gail Miller over something silly. Then Heather learned she had lost out to Rachel Feldman for the title role of "Alice in Wonderland" in the school play after Heather thought for sure she would be picked for the lead.

When she came home from school that day, Heather dashed into her room in tears and threw herself on the bed. She was feeling about as low as she'd ever felt. To make matters worse, Tracy was on the phone, and their mother, a real estate salesperson, was still busy at work, so Heather had no one to comfort her.

In the middle of her crying jag, she experienced an odd sensation. A warmth. A feeling that someone who cared was by her side. Heather felt as though she actually was being held and comforted by invisible arms. *Oh, that's stupid,* she told herself. *I guess I want Mom's arms around me more than I thought. I wish she was home now.*

* * *

Heather was constantly on the go. At school, she was captain of the cheerleading squad and ran her friend Gail's campaign for class president. In her free time, she practiced ballet and volunteered at a nearby nursing home for the elderly. To those who knew her, Heather was bright, upbeat, and sweet.

But shortly after her twelfth birthday, Heather went through a period when she felt down. She sported a full set of new braces on her teeth and was in a growth spurt that made her the tallest girl in her class. She felt awkward and homely—even though she was neither.

It was precisely at this emotional low point when Heather experienced an unforgettable moment that made her believe once and for all that this comforting presence—this gentle ghost—was for real.

Feeling sorry for herself, the sad-faced girl looked into the mirror of her dressing table and complained out loud, "I feel ugly, I look ugly, and I'm getting a pimple on my forehead. What a geek! And don't you dare open your mouth, Heather. The boys are going to tease you and call you 'brace face' and 'metal mouth.'"

She grabbed long strands of hair from both sides of her head and held them straight out. "My hair! It looks so awful. This isn't a bad hair day. It's a bad hair life. I hate it!" She slumped over her table and burst into tears.

But then Heather felt a pair of warm tender hands gently caressing her head. She could feel the fingers running softly through her hair. "Mmmmmm, that feels good," said Heather. She looked up into the mirror expecting to see her mother standing over her. But no one was there. Yet she could plainly see the strands lifting from her scalp as if invisible fingers were playing with her hair.

She blinked once, then twice, to make sure she wasn't imagining this incredible scene. For a fleeting moment, she wanted to scream. But then she felt an overwhelming sense of calm, a sense that she was being comforted by a kind gentle spirit—a spirit that Heather believed was the one she had sensed since early childhood.

Heather's mind quickly fluttered with questions: *Who are you? Where did you come from? Why are you here?* But before Heather could blurt out a word, she no longer felt the invisible hands on her hair. She looked around, not really expecting to see anything, but hoping anyway that the ghost would make itself known.

"Whoever you are, thank you," she said out loud. "That felt so good."

Just then, Heather's mother walked into the room. "Who are you talking to, honey?"

Heather didn't want her mom to think she was crazy. So she said, "No one, Mom. I'm just talking to myself."

"Are you all right? You look very pale."

"I'm feeling a little down right now," said Heather.

"If there's anything you want to talk about . . ."

"No, that's all right. Uh, Mom? Do you believe in ghosts?"

"No, dear, I don't. Why, do you?"

"Yes, I sure do."

Over the next few months, Heather would lie in bed at night and whisper to the spirit, "If you're out there, let me see you. Or at least send me a clue so that I know you really exist."

She waited patiently, but she didn't receive any message. No lights flickered by themselves. No strange noises were heard.

* * *

Shortly before she turned 13, Heather came down with a bad case of the flu. She couldn't hold anything in her stomach, her bones ached, and her fever soared. The flu virus had spread into her ears and messed up her balance. She couldn't crawl out of bed without feeling like she was on a tilt-a-whirl carnival ride. She could barely sit up in bed without feeling dizzy.

"Is there anything I can get you?" asked her mother.

"Something to put me out of my misery," she moaned.

"I've given you all the medication I can, sweetheart. Just try to get some rest. Let's hope the fever will break soon. I'll be downstairs working on a contract. I'll check in on you later. Now close your eyes." Her mother kissed her hot forehead and shut the door.

Heather tossed and turned until she moaned out loud, "I wish I were dead."

"No you don't, dear. You should never wish for such an awful thing."

Heather, her eyes still closed, didn't quite recognize the voice. "Mom, is that you?"

There was no answer. But Heather felt someone sit on the edge of the bed by her pillow and, with a gentle hand, stroke her hair. Heather knew immediately just by the touch that the kind spirit had once again paid her a visit. Heather opened her eyes, not expecting to see anything. To her surprise, she saw a woman gazing at her.

Heather had never seen this woman before, yet she felt she had known the stranger all her life. Heather stared at the woman for the longest time. She had soft violet eyes brimming with love. Smooth, flawless skin the tone of the Goodens' ivory-colored china. Short-cropped blond hair molded in a series of waves that barely reached her ears. Slender lips angled into a sweet smile.

She wore a high-necked white blouse with slightly puffed sleeves and a long dark skirt. She reminded Heather of the kind of woman pictured in her American history book around the time of the Great Depression over 60 years ago. She certainly wasn't dressed for the present day.

"Who are you?" Heather asked.

"Shhhhh," answered the woman, as she continued to stroke Heather's head.

"That feels nice," murmured Heather. Heather's body, which had been tense from the aches and pains caused by the fever and flu, began to relax.

The woman hummed a tune. Heather didn't recognize it, but it sounded like a nursery rhyme. Heather's breathing became less labored and the pain seemed to ease. "You've been here before, haven't you?" Heather asked.

The woman smiled and nodded.

"I've felt your presence before. Like when I'm really sad or really sick. That is you, isn't it?"

Again, the woman nodded.

"I have so many questions to ask you."

Heather tried to sit up, but the woman whispered, "Hush, my sweet." She gently put her hand on Heather's forehead and guided her head back to the pillow.

"Please talk to me," begged Heather.

The woman cocked her head the way a mother does when she looks lovingly at her baby in the crib. She started to say something, but instead she slowly eased off the side of the bed and stood up.

"Don't go. Please don't go," said Heather, beginning to cry.

The woman pulled a pink linen hanky out of her skirt pocket and wiped the tears from Heather's eyes. Heather clutched the woman's hand and felt a strange tingling sensation before it slipped out of her grasp.

The woman took a couple of steps backward and blew Heather a kiss. And then she simply faded away.

Heather sat up in bed and rubbed her eyes. She was immediately hit with a dizzy spell and fell back onto the pillow. Then she slipped into a restful sleep.

When Heather awoke, she knew someone was sitting on the side of her bed. She opened her eyes, hoping to see the woman again. "Oh, Mom, it's you."

"Were you expecting someone else?"

"Oh, sorry, Mom, but I had the weirdest dream. At least, I think it was a dream." Heather wasn't sure. Even though she was convinced that a gentle spirit had visited her in the past, she had never seen the ghost before this day. Maybe it was a dream. "Mom, the woman in my dream looked like she was from Grandma's time and in her twenties. She sat on my bed and stroked my hair and then she just vanished."

"It was probably the medication," said her mother. "It can trigger some wild dreams. How do you feel?"

"A little bit better. I'm not quite so dizzy. Now about this dream. It seemed so real but —" Heather stopped in mid-sentence. Laying on the sheet next to her left hand was a pink linen hanky with a lace border. She picked it up and examined it closely. Sewn in one corner was a purple flower and in the opposite corner the initials M.A.T., also in purple. "Mom, this is the hanky the woman left behind! That means it wasn't a dream at all. It was real!"

"Now, dear, you know that's impossible." Her mother took the hanky from Heather and fingered it. "Beautiful embroidery. Nice quality. Something that Grandma would have used. You must have found it in Grandma's trunk."

"No, Mom. That's not what happened. I got it from this woman and her initials are M.A.T."

* * *

When Heather recovered from the flu, she returned to school and to her volunteer work at the nearby nursing home. She enjoyed spending time with the elderly, taking wheelchair-bound Mr. Michaels on an outing through the park, writing a letter for Mrs. McAfferty, and listening to Mrs. Palmer talk about "the good old days." Mrs. Palmer was 86 years old and in failing health, but her mind remained sharp. She was a living history book.

"Why, I can remember, as plain as yesterday, when Charles A. Lindbergh made the first solo nonstop flight across the Atlantic Ocean," Mrs. Palmer told Heather. "That was in 1927. Back then, flying alone from New York to Paris was an amazing feat—more daring than flying to the moon with all that fancy technology.

"Lindbergh flew on courage and faith in himself. He didn't need to rely on scientists and engineers and experts in big control rooms. Heather, it was so exciting for me because I was there in New York at the ticker-tape parade for Lindbergh when he returned to a hero's welcome. My, what a sight! Tons and tons of confetti falling from the sky."

Mrs. Palmer's account was interrupted by a sneezing

fit. "Heather, would you be a dear and go into the top left-hand drawer and get me a handkerchief?"

Heather opened the drawer, reached in, and startled the elderly woman by exclaiming, "This is unbelievable!" On top of several neatly folded handkerchiefs was a pink linen hanky with lace trim, a purple flower, and the initials M.A.T.! Heather pulled it out and excitedly asked, "Mrs. Palmer, where did you get this?"

Mrs. Palmer looked fondly at the hanky and said, "I have about a half dozen of these. They belonged to my sister Martha Ann. She was such a sweet loving person."

"What happened to her?"

"Oh, she lived a tragic life cut short by the cruelest fate of all—a broken heart."

Heather eagerly pulled up a chair next to Mrs. Palmer. "Please, tell me more."

"Martha Ann was five years older than me. A very pretty woman both inside and out. She married Joseph Taylor —"

"Martha Ann Taylor . . . M.A.T." said Heather. "Those are the initials on the hanky."

"That's right. Anyway, Joseph was a banker, and they built a beautiful house over on Lakewood Avenue sometime in the early 1920s."

"That's unreal! I live on Lakewood!"

"If I recall, it was one house off of Russell Avenue."

"So is mine! 205 Lakewood."

"I don't remember the address, but it's a two-story brick house —"

"With two chimneys on each end?" Heather asked.

"Why, yes. I believe so."

"Mrs. Palmer, that's my house!"

"Goodness gracious if that doesn't tickle my insides."

Heather's heart was pounding now. She felt like a detective moments away from solving a mystery. "Don't stop now. What happened to Martha Ann?"

"My dear child, it's a very sad story. All Martha Ann dreamed about was raising children and being a good mother. Well, she gave birth to a daughter, Louise, who was named after our mother. My how she loved that baby. Rocking her in the cradle, singing nursery rhymes, pampering her. Martha Ann was such a wonderful mother. But . . ." She sighed and shook her head. "Baby Louise contracted yellow fever and died before her first birthday.

"Martha Ann was beside herself with grief. She wouldn't eat or sleep. But her husband Joseph and I managed to help her get over her pain. Two years later, she had another girl, Rebecca. Unfortunately, Rebecca was a sickly baby. She was only six months old when she died of a fever too. Poor Martha Ann. She loved those babies so much.

"After Rebecca's death, Martha Ann hardly ever went outside the house. She never smiled. She'd spend hours upon hours alone in the nursery, aching to care for a child. But she was afraid to have another baby for fear that it too would die. When she lost her babies, she lost her will to live. Martha Ann never made it to her 28th birthday. Officially, she died of pneumonia. But I think she died of a broken heart."

"How sad," said Heather, trying to hold back her tears. She reached over and touched the old woman's arm. "I'm sorry to ask you questions about your sister, but I almost feel like I know her." Heather's mind was racing now at the thought of what she would learn next. "Mrs. Palmer, was the nursery in an upstairs room on the east side of the house?"

"I believe it was. The one facing east to catch the morning sun."

"That's my bedroom!"

Heather's heart was pounding wildly now. There was only one more piece of evidence she needed to confirm the identity of the ghost. "Do you have a picture of Martha Ann?"

"Look in the closet on the top shelf. There should be a red photo album." With trembling hands, Heather brought the album to her and placed it on Mrs. Palmer's lap. Then Heather eagerly looked over the old lady's shoulder.

Flipping through the pages, Mrs. Palmer stopped at a yellowed photo of over a dozen people posing in their Sunday best. "This photo of our family reunion was taken about 1925—a short while after Martha Ann was married. Now let's see . . ."

Heather's eyes quickly focused on one particular woman. The facial features, the hair, the eyes, and that smile. It was the very same person who had been at her bedside. Heather pointed to the woman and declared, "That's her! That's Martha Ann!"

"You're absolutely right! How did you know?"

Heather threw her arms around Mrs. Palmer and gave her a big hug. "It's a long story," Heather said. "But I'll tell you this much. Martha Ann may have died a long time ago, but her spirit is still very much alive!"

THE HAUNTED PLAYHOUSE

**I**f George Hill had to do it all over again, he never would have built a walk-in playhouse for his seven-year-old daughter Melissa. But then, who knew it would turn into a creepy haunted house?

George, a carpenter, decided to build the playhouse for his only daughter in the backyard shortly after the Hills moved into their home. In one corner of the yard, which was surrounded by a tall wooden fence, sat a crumbling, weathered toolshed. The tar-paper roof sagged, both windows were busted, and the door was rotting.

"Princess," said Melissa's father, "I think with a little imagination and lots of hard work, we can turn that poor excuse for a shack into a beautiful playhouse for you."

Melissa threw her arms around her father's waist and said, "Daddy, you're the best!"

With Melissa and her mother Maryanne helping out, George replaced the old wood, put down vinyl tile over the cement slab, and installed two new windows. He added a higher roof complete with a fake chimney so that the ceiling was tall enough inside for any young child to stand.

Melissa then chose the colors for her playhouse. Bright yellow walls inside and out, a red door, a blue roof, a purple chimney, and green trim around the windows. Inside her playhouse, she arranged her play table and chairs, a plastic toy kitchen, several dolls and teddy bears, a dollhouse, and a toy chest.

"It's so pretty!" Melissa said after she had finished decorating her new playhouse. "Mommy, Daddy, let's have a tea party." The curly-haired, dimple-faced girl made them sit on the floor where she served them orange juice in tiny teacups. "I love my playhouse. It's just perfect."

But it wasn't really.

Everyone overlooked the first hint that there was something strange about the playhouse. During the tea party, George finished a roll of film by taking four pictures of Melissa. When the roll was developed, all the pictures came out, but there seemed to be something wrong with the ones taken in the playhouse. Each of those photos showed the faint image of another girl standing behind Melissa. The girl, clad in a white ruffled dress, sported bangs and a white ribbon in her shoulder-length blond hair. Although the image wasn't in sharp focus, everyone noticed her piercing dark eyes and menacing sneer.

"Who's that, Daddy?" asked Melissa.

"I don't know, honey," he replied. "Do you know, Maryanne?"

"I don't recognize her as anyone in the neighborhood or at school," said Maryanne. "How did she get in the photo?"

"It must be a double exposure," he explained. "Remember when we took pictures at the county fair last week? I guess the camera failed to advance and took the last four pictures on the same frame. Why or how we ended up taking photos of this little girl I don't know."

"Whoever she is, she doesn't look very sweet," said Maryanne. "In fact, she looks kind of . . . well . . . spooky."

"Kind of like a ghost," added Melissa.

If she only knew.

* * *

A few days later, Melissa walked into the kitchen, pouting. "Mommy, somebody was in my playhouse and messed up my dollhouse."

"What do you mean, honey?"

"The furniture in the nursery is now in the living room, the dining room set is in the parents' bedroom, and some of the kitchen stuff is gone."

"Gone? You've got to be careful. Some of that is play furniture I had when I was a little girl. You were with some of your friends yesterday in the playhouse. Were any of them playing with your dollhouse furniture?"

"Yes. But when we left, everything was just right. Today, the dollhouse was all changed inside. Someone went into my playhouse without asking—and that's wrong."

Two days later, Melissa was by herself in the play-house when she thought she heard a young girl whisper,

"Bad girl. Bad girl." Melissa peered outside, but didn't see anyone. *It sounds like it's coming from inside,* she thought. *But how can it? I'm all alone.* Melissa listened carefully and tried to pinpoint the location of the whispering voice.

"Bad girl. Baaad girl."

Following the voice, Melissa dropped to her hands and knees and looked inside her dollhouse. The voice seemed to be coming from an upstairs bedroom! Melissa didn't know what shocked her more—the voice or the scene in the tiny bedroom. The furniture had been destroyed. The cute canopy over the bed lay torn in shreds, the floor lamp was snapped in two, the legs on the bed and end tables were broken, and the drawers from the dresser were scattered throughout the room.

"Bad girl. Baaad girl."

Melissa let out a high-pitched scream and ran out of the playhouse. "Mommy! Mommy!" she shouted as she threw open the kitchen door. "Someone's in my dollhouse!"

"You mean your *play*house?"

"No, my *doll*house!" Grabbing her mother's hand, she pleaded, "Come with me. Hurry." Melissa led her into the playhouse and made her kneel down in front of the dollhouse and listen. "I heard a voice say 'bad girl,'" Melissa declared. "And it was coming from that bedroom."

"I don't hear anything," said her mother. Then, becoming upset over the damaged dollhouse furniture, her mother snapped, "What happened to the bedroom set? I told you to be careful."

"Somebody broke it," said Melissa with tears welling in her eyes. "But not me."

"Who was in here with you?"

"No one, except maybe the girl I heard."

"Melissa," her mother said in a voice rising with anger, "Are you telling me that the person responsible for this is a tiny invisible girl who lives in your dollhouse? A girl who no one can see and only you can hear?"

It did sound silly to Melissa, but she had no other explanation. Frustrated that her mother wouldn't believe her, Melissa burst into tears and ran out of the playhouse.

That night, after their daughter had been tucked into bed, George and Maryanne Hill fretted over what to do.

"She's always been so careful with her things," said Maryanne. "She denies breaking her dollhouse furniture and says none of her friends could have done it either. And now she claims to have heard a voice say 'bad girl.' I'm worried about her, George."

"Sounds like that voice is nothing more than a guilty conscience talking," he said. "Maybe we should teach her a lesson. We'll take the dollhouse away from her for a week."

With his flashlight, he went inside the playhouse and noticed that, other than the broken bedroom furniture, everything else in the dollhouse looked fine. As he lifted it up, he heard a little girl's voice whisper threateningly, "You'll be sorry."

At first, George shrugged it off. *It must be the neighbor's TV set I'm hearing,* he thought. *But it sure does sound like it's coming from this dollhouse.* As he carried the dollhouse into the garage, he heard a slight *crunch, crunch,* but he couldn't detect where the noise came from. He then set the dollhouse on the shelf by his workbench and glanced inside. "Well, I'll be darned," he muttered with surprise. Now the stairway and all the living room furniture were busted—as though they had been crushed by an invisible fist.

"I can't explain it," he told Maryanne minutes later. "When I first looked inside the dollhouse, only the furniture in the bedroom had been broken. I was careful when I carried it into the garage, and I didn't bang into anything. There's no way the stairs and living room furniture should have broken up."

"This is crazy," she said. "There has to be an explanation."

"And I hope there's an explanation for something else," he added. "As I was carrying the dollhouse into the garage, I thought I heard a little girl's voice say, 'You'll be sorry.'"

"George, not you too?" said Maryanne, shaking her head in disbelief.

* * *

A few days later Melissa was in her playhouse, combing the hair of one of her favorite dolls, when she heard that same whispering voice hiss, "You're no good."

Melissa looked around and asked, "Who said that?"

"You're in trouble," uttered the voice.

"Who are you?" asked Melissa, searching behind her toy chest. "And where are you?"

"Big, big trouble."

When Melissa finally discovered where the voice was

coming from, she froze. The voice was coming from the mouth of one of her favorite dolls! It was a large plastic doll she had named Tiffany. Tiffany's lips didn't move but there was no doubt in Melissa's mind that her doll was talking to her.

"You're baaad," said Tiffany, slowly drawing out the last word. "You must be punished."

"Shut up!" snapped Melissa. Then she threw the doll into her toy chest, slammed the lid down, and ran back into the house.

"Mommy!" she said breathlessly. "My doll Tiffany talked to me! And she wasn't very nice."

"Oh, really?" replied her mother, dismissing it as a child's fantasy. "And what did she say?"

Melissa could tell from the tone of her mother's voice that she didn't believe her. "I'm not kidding. Tiffany said I was bad and that I must be punished."

"Did you do anything that would make her say such a thing?"

"No I didn't. Mommy, really, she talked to me!"

"Just like the voice in the dollhouse?"

Melissa stormed out of the kitchen and ran back into the playhouse. She blinked twice. She clearly remembered throwing Tiffany in the toy chest. Yet there was Tiffany sitting in a chair!

"How did you get out?" Melissa asked.

"How dare you!" hissed Tiffany. "You will pay for this."

Melissa grabbed the doll and twisted its head around until it fell off. Then she yanked on the arms and legs until they popped out of their sockets. She picked up the parts and threw them in the garbage can. "No more Tiffany!" Melissa declared.

Later, after putting Melissa to bed for the evening, Maryanne took out the trash. In the twilight, Maryanne opened the garbage can and immediately spotted parts of Tiffany inside. *Oh, no!* she thought. *Now Melissa has ripped apart one of her favorite dolls. What's happening to her? Why is she so destructive? I hope she didn't tear up her other dolls.*

She scurried into the playhouse and breathed a sigh of relief. All the dolls were neatly in place. As she closed the door behind her and started back to the house, Maryanne thought she heard a little girl's faint voice warn, "You're going to get it!"

That's just great, Maryanne told herself. *Now I'm hearing things.*

After school the next day, Melissa and two friends skipped over to the playhouse. When Melissa opened the door, she took one look inside—and shrieked in anguish. "My dolls! My teddy bears!" She burst into tears.

Hearing her daughter wailing, Maryanne ran toward the playhouse. "What's wrong, sweetheart?"

Trying hard to catch her breath, Melissa said between sobs, "Someone killed all my dolls!"

Her mother opened the playhouse door and gasped at the sight. Heads, arms, and legs had been ripped off Melissa's dolls and scattered all over the floor. Eyes and noses had been torn off the teddy bears and stuffing lay in every corner.

But the most chilling sight of all was Melissa's doll

Samantha. Samantha was dangling from the ceiling light, her neck in a noose made from one of Melissa's hair ribbons.

"Who would do this, Mommy? Who could be that mean?"

"I don't know, sweetheart. All I know is that this person is sick in the head—very sick."

Maryanne was hit with a double dose of emotions—anger toward the person who destroyed the dolls and dollhouse furniture and guilt for wrongly believing that her daughter had been responsible.

* * *

"It couldn't be any of her friends," George told Maryanne after dinner that night. "They're too small to climb the fence, and the backyard gate is always locked. The only way to get to the playhouse is through our house. And no little kid is going to sneak in here without us knowing it."

"That means it had to be an older kid or some weird person in the neighborhood," said Maryanne. "But who?"

"I don't know, but I'm putting a lock on the playhouse door. What is this world coming to when a little girl can't play without fear in her own backyard?"

A week had passed before Melissa returned to the playhouse. She decided to make pretend soup by pouring water from the garden hose into a pot and placing the pot on her toy plastic stove. As she cut up imaginary vegetables and put them in the water, Melissa's toy ring slipped off her finger and plopped into the pot. She stuck her hand in the water to retrieve it and let out an anguished cry.

"My hand! My hand!" she cried out in pain. "I've burned my hand!" The skin on her hand began to turn red. "Mommy! Mommy! Come quick!"

Her mother dashed out to the playhouse. "What happened, Melissa?"

"I put my hand in the water and it got burned."

Maryanne stuck her finger in the water and pulled it out quickly. "Ouch! It's so hot it's almost boiling. Where did you get this hot water?"

"From the hose. But the water was cold when I put it on my play stove."

"This doesn't make any sense," said her mother. "Your stove is just a plastic toy. It has no heating unit. Come on, you poor darling, let's go back to the house so I can make your hand feel better."

As they started to leave, they heard the eerie voice of a little girl whisper, "I hope it hurts."

"Mommy, I'm scared," said Melissa.

"Princess, I am too."

* * *

"No one goes into the playhouse until we get to the bottom of this," declared George later that night.

"I've been doing a lot of thinking," said Maryanne. "And what I'm thinking sounds crazy, but it makes sense too." She pulled out the photos that showed the faint image of a little girl. "What if this isn't a double exposure? What if this is a photo of a ghost of a child?"

"What are you saying, Maryanne? That the playhouse is haunted?"

"Why not? We all heard the strange voice of a little girl in the playhouse—and even in the dollhouse—that

72

no one could see. She could be the girl in the photo. Tell me those eyes and that sinister look on her face don't give you the chills."

"That could explain the smashed dollhouse furniture and the torn-up dolls when no one else was inside," he said. "And I suppose a supernatural force could heat up water on a toy stove."

"So what do we do now, call Ghostbusters?" she asked only half in jest.

"I know what I want to do. First thing in the morning, I'm getting out my trusty sledgehammer and —"

"George, wait, please," said Maryanne. "Let's try to find out who this ghost is and why she's haunting the playhouse. If we're not careful, she might wind up haunting our house. Maybe the neighbors know something about the history of this place that could help us."

The next day, Maryanne talked with Mrs. Peterson, who had lived in the neighborhood longer than almost anyone else. After listening to Maryanne describe the bizarre happenings in the playhouse, Mrs. Peterson said, "Brace yourself, hon. Have I got a story for you."

Mrs. Peterson poured both of them a cup of coffee and began. "About 20 years ago, Earl and Helen Latham lived in the house you're in now. They were mean cold people, not sociable at all. They had a daughter, Misty, who they physically abused. For punishment, they'd take her out into the tool shed—which you turned into a playhouse—and hit her with a leather strap. We could hear her parents yelling mean things to her. We called the cops on them several times, but the Lathams always managed to weasel out of going to jail.

"One day, when Misty was about eight years old, she was getting punished in the tool shed. While struggling to get free, she jarred loose a shelf and fell. It was terrible. A 50-pound sack of cement landed on her, broke her neck, and she died. This time, the parents went to jail.

"After that, there were rumors that the tool shed was haunted. The next two owners of the house used to complain that someone was moving their tools and things in the shed—even hiding them. And the owners claimed they heard the voice of a little girl saying mean, nasty things. We all began to wonder if perhaps it wasn't the ghost of Misty Latham."

"Why didn't you tell us this before?" asked Maryanne.

"I'm sorry I didn't. But you, George, and Melissa were so thrilled to have your first house that I didn't want to ruin it for you. I didn't know you had turned the tool shed into a playhouse until after it was built, and I didn't have the heart to tell you then."

"There's one more thing," said Maryanne. She pulled out the photos of Melissa that showed the ghostly image of a little girl behind her. "Is this Misty?"

Mrs. Peterson put on her glasses and studied the photos. She clasped her hands to her face and declared, "My goodness! That's Misty! Why, that looks like the very dress she was buried in."

"Now I understand why this ghost in the playhouse is so mean," said Maryanne. "Everything she ever said to us probably were phrases she heard her parents say to her in the tool shed when she was being punished. And the ghost was doing those terrible things to Melissa because often abused children become abusers themselves."

That evening, after they assumed Melissa was asleep upstairs, Maryanne told George about her stunning conversation with Mrs. Peterson. "Okay, then it's agreed," said George. "I'll tear down the playhouse tomorrow."

"No, you can't!" shouted Melissa from the bottom of the stairway. She had sneaked down and was listening to her parents talk in the living room about the ghost. "I heard everything you said. I don't want you to knock down the playhouse."

"But why not, Princess?" asked George.

"My playhouse is so pretty, and I really like it. Besides, I feel sad for that little girl."

"I do too, George," added Maryanne. She thought a moment, snapped her fingers, and said, "I have an idea about how to make the playhouse safe again."

The next day, Maryanne and Melissa entered the playhouse and were startled at the sight. The room had been trashed. The table and chairs had been overturned, and toys were scattered everywhere.

"Misty," Maryanne called out. "That wasn't a nice thing to do." After they straightened up the room, Maryanne said, "Misty, we know all about you—how you were a sweet little girl who was abused and died in an accident in the tool shed. We feel very sorry for you and sad that you didn't have the love you deserved. But you can't go around scaring Melissa and destroying her things. That's not right. You're dead, and you must leave here. This is Melissa's playhouse now."

Melissa, clutching a Raggedy Ann doll, added,

"Mommy explained to me what happened to you. I feel bad for you, Misty, I really do. I wish you had nice parents like I have. They gave me this doll." Melissa held it up and then gently placed it on a chair. "I'm putting it on this chair. It's for you to play with. Just be nice to it, okay?"

With that said, mother and daughter left. They didn't know what to expect when they entered the playhouse the following morning. But as they stepped inside, they gave a big sigh of relief. The room was just as they had left it.

"I think she's left for good," said Maryanne. "Everything is in its place, nice and tidy."

"Mommy, look!" said Melissa, pointing to the chair where she had placed the Raggedy Ann doll the day before. "The doll, it's gone!"

The playhouse was never haunted again.

THE POND OF DEATH

Jeremy Sanders will never, ever disobey a "No Trespassing" sign again. Not after his terrifying life-and-death struggle at Norquist Pond.

Jeremy, 14, was spending two weeks of his summer vacation with his cousin Kyle Barnes, who lived in a small country town in Minnesota. The boys got along great because they were the same age and had the same interests—especially fishing at nearby Lake Swenson. The only difference between the two was that Jeremy liked to get up early while Kyle enjoyed sleeping late.

One day, at the crack of dawn, Jeremy decided to get in some fishing before Kyle woke up. So Jeremy hopped on his cousin's motor scooter and headed down the road that led to Lake Swenson five miles away.

Fingers of fog stretched across the countryside in the cool pine-scented air. As he reached the crest of a hill, Jeremy spotted a boy about 12 years old walking alongside the road. The stocky, brown-haired youth wore a sleeveless yellow T-shirt, blue cut-offs, and black high-tops. He carried a dented metal tackle box in his left hand and rested a fishing pole and net over his right shoulder.

Jeremy pulled over and said, "Hi! Going to the lake?"

The boy nodded and said, "I'm going just past it."

"Want a ride?"

"Okay, thanks." The boy hopped onto the motor scooter, placed the tackle box on his lap, and wrapped his left arm around Jeremy's waist. The boy's pale bare arm felt like ice to Jeremy even though Jeremy was wearing a jacket.

"My name is Jeremy."

"I'm Tommy."

As they sped off, Jeremy asked, "So what are you fishing for?"

The answer was not what Jeremy expected: "Revenge."

"What do you mean?"

"I'm going back to Norquist Pond to teach that guy a lesson," replied Tommy. "He made my canoe capsize and I'm not going to let him get away with it. He can't do anything to me anymore."

"Who are you talking about?"

"Lars."

"Who's Lars?"

"You're not from around here, are you?" said Tommy. "Everyone has heard of Lars. He's the bad dude at Norquist Pond. A very bad dude."

"My cousin Kyle told me that nobody is allowed to fish in Norquist Pond."

"That's true," said Tommy. "But it's great fishing there. The problem is Olaf Norquist owns the land, and he doesn't like people using the pond. If Norquist catches you, all he does is yell at you to get out because some bad things have happened at the pond. There aren't any fences around there or anything, just some old 'No Trespassing' signs. I never paid attention to them."

Tommy paused and added, "I guess maybe I should have. Yesterday I found the old man's canoe hidden in the bushes, so I took it out in the pond. That's when Lars got me."

By now, the boys had reached the boat ramp to Lake Swenson. "Well, this is where I plan to fish today," said Jeremy. "Care to join me?"

"No thanks. I'm going on to Norquist Pond. It's only a half mile from here, down that dirt road. If you're not having any luck, you can always try the pond."

"What about Mr. Norquist?"

"Oh, don't worry about him. Just look out for Lars."

"I'll see you later," said Jeremy.

"Probably not."

That's a strange reply, thought Jeremy. *What did he mean by that?* Jeremy took his tackle box out of the motor-scooter basket, turned around, and said, "If you need a lift back . . ." He stopped when he realized that Tommy was nowhere in sight. *Hey, where did he go? There's no way he could have disappeared like that.* Lake Swenson was surrounded by grass and pine trees. But the nearest trees were 20 yards away—too far for the boy to have reached so quickly.

Jeremy shrugged his shoulders and went down to the

edge of the lake and began fishing. Before he felt his first nibble, a caravan of four-wheel-drive trucks from the sheriff's office roared past him with lights flashing and turned onto the dirt road that led to Norquist Pond. *Something big must be going on over there*, thought Jeremy. *I better go check it out.*

Putting his fishing gear away, Jeremy hopped onto his motor scooter and headed over to the pond, which was bustling with activity. Sheriff's deputies hauled flat-bottomed boats into the water while a team of scuba divers formed a line and began swimming out toward the center of the pond.

Jeremy walked around the edge of the water, approached a deputy, and asked, "What's going on?"

"We're searching for a boy who drowned here yesterday. He was fishing in a canoe late in the day when it flipped over. Mr. Norquist saw him struggle and then go under, but the old man was too feeble to swim out and save him. By the time we arrived, the sun was going down and we couldn't find the kid. There's been no sign of the body yet. The strange thing is that Tommy was a good swimmer."

"Are you saying a boy named Tommy drowned here?" asked Jeremy.

"Apparently so," replied the deputy.

"Was this kid about 12 years old with short brown hair? Was he wearing cut-off jeans and a yellow T-shirt?"

The deputy flipped through his notes and said, "Right on the money. How did you know?"

"I saw him this morning! In fact, I gave him a ride on my motor scooter."

"What? Are you sure?"

"I'm positive. He said his name was Tommy and that he had to go back to the lake to teach some guy named Lars a lesson. He said that Lars had capsized his canoe."

The deputy clicked on his walkie talkie and said, "Sheriff, I've got a kid here who says he gave Tommy Hilton a lift to the lake—this morning! That's what he says. Sure, it seems impossible, but you never know —"

The conversation was interrupted by shouts from a scuba diver out in the pond. "We've found him!" He and another scuba diver then dragged the lifeless body of a boy into the boat. When the boat reached the bank, Jeremy took a glance at the body—and shook with shock. He couldn't believe his eyes. It was the same boy he had picked up less than two hours earlier!

"What was this about seeing Tommy this morning?" the now angry deputy snapped at Jeremy.

"I—I—I swear, he was the one I gave a ride to today," Jeremy stammered. "Honest."

"Look, kid, I can tell from looking at the body that he's been dead for at least 12 hours." He glowered at Jeremy. "What's your name?"

"Jeremy Sanders."

"You're new here, aren't you."

"Yes, sir. I'm visiting my cousin, Kyle Barnes."

The deputy wrote Jeremy's name down in his note-book and snapped, "I think you'd best get out of here right now before I run you in for making false statements during an ongoing investigation."

Jeremy wanted to protest, but he knew it wouldn't do any good. So—confused, upset, and scared—he climbed onto his motor scooter and sped back to his cousin's house.

* * *

When Jeremy finished explaining to Uncle Phil, Aunt Diane, and Kyle what had happened to him earlier that morning, no one scoffed at him. Instead, they seemed to believe him—even though his story sounded so incredible.

"Dad, do you suppose Lars killed Tommy?" asked Kyle.

"I'm beginning to think so," Phil replied.

"Murder?" gasped Jeremy.

"Oh, Phil, don't start that talk about Lars," said Diane.

"Another strange death, and you want to ignore it?" Phil countered.

"I don't know what to believe," she admitted. "Did Jeremy really see Tommy's ghost? Did Lars kill Tommy?"

"Just who is Lars anyway?" asked Jeremy. "That kid kept talking about Lars, saying he was bad. What's the story about him?"

"Norquist Pond may look peaceful," said his uncle, "but some people around here are convinced it's haunted by the evil spirit of a bully named Lars who lived in town in the early 1900s. Every once in a while someone dies in the pond under strange circumstances. And people blame it on Lars.

"The story goes that Lars was a big, burly teenager who liked to bully the kids in town. Everyone was afraid of him. He would steal food from their lunch pails at school, scare their horses, rip up their homework, things like that. He was a bad kid.

"The other kids decided to teach Lars a lesson. About a dozen of them sneaked up behind him one day while he was fishing at the pond. They threw a burlap bag over his head and tackled him. Then they tied his hands and feet with rope.

"The boys wrapped another rope around his chest and waist and tossed it over a thick tree branch that extended over the pond. They hoisted Lars up so he was dangling above the water. They dunked him by releasing some of the rope until he was underwater, and then they yanked on the rope and pulled him up. They did this a couple of times, all the while demanding that he cry 'uncle' and say he was sorry for all the mean things he did to them. But Lars refused. He just kept yelling at them.

"So they left him dangling from the branch above the water and told him they'd be back in an hour. But when they returned, he wasn't there. At some point while they were gone, the big branch holding Lars had snapped off, sending him into the water. Since he was all tied up, he couldn't swim. The boys dove into the pond and pulled Lars out. They quickly untied him and took the burlap bag off his head. Unfortunately he was already dead.

"In their panic, the boys decided to make it look like an accident. They dragged his body out into the middle of the pond and let it sink. The kids then swore themselves to eternal secrecy, promising they would never tell what really happened.

"A couple of days later, the authorities found Lars' body. They suspected foul play, and eventually the boys confessed. Naturally, they didn't mean to kill Lars or even hurt him. They just wanted to teach him a lesson. Justice being what it was back then, Lars' death was ruled an accidental drowning."

"Here's where it gets really bizarre," added Kyle, interrupting his father's account. "There have been several mysterious deaths in the pond over the years. You know, like a good swimmer suddenly goes under and doesn't come up. Or somebody drowns in one end of the pond, and they find his body at the other end even though there's no current. Some people think that Lars' evil spirit caused these deaths as a way of getting even with the town."

"Wow," said Jeremy in wide-eyed amazement. "Do you think Lars was responsible for Tommy's death?"

"Could be," Kyle replied. "Tommy knew how to swim. He shouldn't have drowned."

"Okay, that's enough talk about Lars," said Aunt Diane. "Jeremy, I hope you're not too upset about all this."

"I don't know what I am right now," he replied. "It's not every day you give a ghost a ride or learn that another ghost goes around drowning people."

"Although I believe you, let's keep your experience with Tommy's ghost quiet," said Aunt Diane. "This is a small town and people will talk."

"That's fine with me," said Jeremy.

"Good," she said. "There's one more thing: Kyle and Jeremy, I want you both to promise me that you won't go swimming in that pond."

"I promise," said Jeremy.

"Me too," added Kyle, crossing his fingers behind his back.

Near the end of his vacation, on the hottest day of the year, Jeremy and Kyle went fishing at Lake Swenson. But as the sun climbed higher in the sky, neither teen had hooked a fish.

"This is a bummer," said Jeremy. "What do you say we quit?"

"No way," said Kyle. "I haven't been shut out all summer. Let's try another fishing hole that's never let me down." The two got on Kyle's motor scooter and rode along a bumpy trail for about ten minutes, past a bullet-riddled "No Trespassing" sign, until they reached the sandy edge of a tiny lake.

"Say, isn't this Norquist Pond?" asked Jeremy.

"Yes," Kyle replied with a mischievous grin. "We're on the far side of the pond. The fishing is always great here."

"How do you know?"

"I come here from time to time. I always catch at least one keeper."

"I don't think this is a good idea," said Jeremy.

"We promised my mom that we'd catch dinner. This is the best fishing spot in the county. Nothing can happen to us here. That is, unless you're afraid that Lars might jump out of the water and grab you by the throat and drag you under." Kyle leaped for Jeremy and playfully wrestled him to the ground. The two rolled around, laughing, before Kyle pinned Jeremy.

"Okay, okay," said Jeremy, catching his breath. "We'll fish here—but only until we catch enough for dinner."

An hour later, they each had reeled in three nice-sized large-mouth bass. By now, the sun was beating down and sweat was dripping off the boys. "Man, it's got to be in the mid-nineties," said Kyle. He peeled off his shoes, socks, and shirt and jumped into the water.

"What are you doing?" asked Jeremy with surprise.

"It's hot. I'm sweaty and dirty and I'm cooling off."

"But we promised your mom —"

"We promised not to go swimming. I'm just wading. It's not like I'm going out into the middle or anything." Kyle splashed around in water up to his waist. "Man, this feels great. Come on in, Jeremy." Kyle slapped the water with his hand, spraying Jeremy.

"Hey, you dweeb!" Jeremy began ripping off his shirt and shoes. "Now you're going to get it!" Jeremy jumped into the water and tried to grab Kyle, who was now backstroking farther away from the bank. The boys were laughing and joking around as Jeremy chased Kyle further out into the pond until he caught him by the foot. The two then tried to dunk each other for fun.

After they finally tired out, they tread water and playfully insulted each other. But Jeremy stopped joking when he noticed something weird moving in the pond. Pointing to a spot in the water about 30 yards away, he asked, "Hey, what's that over there?"

Something about six feet long was skimming along the surface with a small wake trailing behind it. "It's too big to be a monster bass or a walleye," said Kyle. "Whatever it is, it's heading straight toward us."

Before they could swim away from its path, the mysterious object closed in on them swiftly and silently. When they finally saw what it was, Jeremy gagged on a mouthful of water from shock while Kyle screamed in terror. Bobbing in the pond directly in front of them was the body of a big, burly teenage boy. He had thick blond hair, blazing blue eyes, and a face red with anger and hate. Jeremy thought at first that they were staring at another drowned body. But the ghastly horror moved on its own, circling the two frightened teens like a shark ready for the kill. Then it slipped beneath the surface.

"Who is that?" shrieked Jeremy. "What is that?"

"It's Lars!" Kyle shouted before disappearing under the water.

"Kyle! Kyle! Where are you?" Jeremy frantically cried out. Jeremy took a deep breath and swam below the surface. He could see that Lars had a hold of Kyle's leg and was trying to drag him toward the bottom. Jeremy grabbed the attacker by the head and twisted until Kyle was freed. Both boys then shot up to the surface and gasped for breath.

"Let's get to shore fast!" yelled Jeremy. He started swimming with all his might when Lars jumped on Jeremy's back and shoved him under. Jeremy clawed desperately at the water but no matter how hard he tried, Jeremy couldn't break Lars' iron grasp that kept him below the surface.

His lungs burning from lack of oxygen, Jeremy twisted and turned his body but still couldn't break free. They were only a couple of feet under the water, but to Jeremy it might as well have been one hundred. *I'm going to die! I'm going to die!* The panic-stricken youth fought the urge to give up—to open his mouth and let the water fill his pain-wracked lungs just so he'd be put out of his misery. *I can't hold out any longer.*

As Jeremy started to lose consciousness, he saw the hull of a red canoe above him. A paddle came crashing down on Lars' head, and Lars' death grip quickly relaxed. Jeremy then felt a hand clasp his arm and lift him to the surface. Gagging, sputtering, and coughing, Jeremy gulped life-giving air into his aching lungs. Then he passed out.

When Jeremy regained consciousness, he found himself sprawled out on the sand. Next to him sat Kyle, leaning against a tree with his head in his hands, trembling and crying.

"I thought I was going to die," said Jeremy, still shaking from his ordeal. "Thanks for saving my life."

"I didn't save your life," replied Kyle, trying to regain his composure. "You saved mine. When I was pulled under by Lars, you freed me and I managed to make it back to the bank. But by then Lars had grabbed you."

"Then who saved me?" asked Jeremy.

Kyle pointed out toward the middle of the pond. "I can't explain it, but there's your answer."

Jeremy took one look and shook his head in awe. "I don't believe what I'm seeing," he said. Paddling away from them in a red canoe was a young boy about 12 years old in a yellow T-shirt. He disappeared into the reeds and was never seen again. And Jeremy and Kyle never again went to Norquist Pond.

THE PORTRAIT FROM BEYOND

**J**ayne Dillard loved to draw portraits.

With her hard-lead pencil and oversized drawing paper, she often sat in the mall and sketched faces of shoppers for her own practice. On weekends the green-eyed, red-haired 13-year-old went down to the local flea market and set up her easel and folding chair under a large umbrella. Then she drew caricatures—funny portraits—of people who paid her $5 a sketch.

Sometimes throughout the summer months, Jayne would go down to Manville Park and spend hours drawing all sorts of people: young mothers pushing strollers, kids skateboarding and in-line skating, couples walking their dogs.

One day, Jayne put her sketch pad and pencils in her backpack along with her favorite sack lunch—a peanut butter and banana sandwich with an apple for dessert and a small bottle of cranberry juice to drink. She hopped on her bike and headed for Manville Park.

I've been to that park so many times, she thought. *I think I know every single person there—and every flower and tree as well. I think I'll try Carlin Park instead.*

She had no idea where that innocent decision would eventually lead her.

When she reached the park, she rode along the bike trail, looking for just the right subject. *I've sketched enough mothers and babies, and kids on skateboards. I want to do something different.* Then she spotted two elderly men up ahead. *Hey, I think I just found my subjects for the day.*

Jayne hopped off her bicycle, propped it up against an iron fence, and studied the men who were about 20 yards away from her. The two senior citizens sat in the shade of a towering oak tree and were playing dominoes on one of the many round cement tables that dotted the park's landscape.

The men looked like they were in their seventies. One was tall, had short gray hair, sported thick glasses, and wore a white short-sleeve shirt, baggy blue shorts, and leather sandals. Sitting opposite him was his companion—a short chubby man with a pear-shaped body, crewcut white hair, and a big nose that he constantly rubbed just before making his next move in dominoes. He wore a Dallas Cowboys T-shirt, red shorts, and sneakers that had seen better days.

Hoping they wouldn't pay any attention to her, Jayne took out her art supplies and sat on the ground with her back against the fence. With her sketch pad propped up against her raised knees, she began to draw. Whenever Jayne sketched in the park, she hoped people wouldn't know she was drawing them, because she wanted to capture her subjects when they were their most natural.

As she sketched them, Jayne noticed a sadness in the old men's eyes. There were few smiles and little laughter. It seemed as though they were just going through the motions, playing dominoes without joy or enthusiasm.

They don't seem very happy, she thought. *Maybe they're sick. I wonder what's wrong.* Jayne looked at her drawing. She wasn't too pleased with it because the faces of the men were so sad. *This drawing looks depressing. I don't like it at all.*

Jayne was just about to put her sketch pad down when she looked up and saw a third elderly man standing a few feet behind the table watching the two old men. He had a distinctive face: a bushy, salt-and-pepper mustache, brown eyes that twinkled, and an engaging smile that never went away even when he took a puff on his stubby cigar. He was bald on top except for the long curly grayish-brown hair that ringed the back of his head from ear to ear. Short and squat, he wore a green golf shirt and red and green plaid pants. He looked like a fun grandfatherly type.

Perfect! thought Jayne. *Now I can put a little life in this drawing. He's just what I needed. A great face.* As she sketched him, she noticed that the two other men seemed to lighten up. They began chuckling and talking with much more animation. But Jayne also found it strange that they were ignoring the third man. In fact, they never said a word to him. They didn't look at him, even though he was only a few feet away from them. The man didn't seem to mind. He just stood there and watched them, still displaying that big warm smile and puffing on his cigar.

As Jayne was finishing up the details of the third man's face, she looked up and was surprised to see that he had left. She looked in both directions, but he was nowhere to be seen.

How could he disappear like that? she wondered. *He was here just a second ago. Darn it, another couple of minutes and I would have finished him right down to the wrinkles in his cheeks. Oh, well, my drawing is good enough.* She turned her attention back to the sketch pad when she heard an old man's scratchy voice.

"Hey, young lady!"

Jayne looked up and saw that the two old men had left their table and were ambling toward her.

"Are you talking to me?" she asked.

"Sure am," said the tall one. "You wouldn't be drawing two old guys, now would you?"

"Well, actually I was drawing both of you. I hope you don't mind."

"My name is Joe and my friend here is Tony," said the short one.

"Hi, I'm Jayne."

"Is it okay if we take a peek at your drawing, Jayne?" asked Tony.

She stood up and turned the sketch pad around so they could see the drawing. Both men stopped in their tracks, then moved closer until their noses practically touched the paper. They stepped back and looked at each other in shock. Their eyes teared up and their lips trembled. That wasn't the reaction Jayne was expecting.

It's not my best work, but I don't think it's that bad, she thought. *Maybe they're insulted because I made them look too sad and too old. Maybe I shouldn't have shown it to them.*

"You, don't like it, do you?" she said.

"No, it's nothing like that, my dear," replied Tony. "It's amazing, truly amazing," he added, his eyes still locked on the sketch.

"It's such an incredible likeness," marveled Joe. He turned to Jayne and asked, "How did you know Eddie?"

"Who's Eddie?" she replied.

"Him," Joe said, pointing to the elderly gentleman in the middle of the drawing. "That's Eddie Vitale."

"It's unbelievable," Tony declared. "You captured him perfectly—the twinkle in his eyes, the curly hair, that brush of a mustache . . ."

"She's even got him smoking one of his smelly cigars."

"Where did you meet Eddie?" asked Joe.

"I've never met him before. I mean, I saw him standing there with you, so I drew him —"

"Hold on a second," said Tony. "Exactly when did you see him?"

"During the last 15 minutes or so," Jayne replied. "You had to have seen him. He was standing only a few feet away from you just like in my drawing. He left a couple of minutes ago. You did see him, didn't you?"

The two men stared at each other with open mouths. "The last time we saw Eddie was at his funeral," Joe said. "Eddie—our dearest friend—died last week!"

Jayne covered her mouth to hide her shock. "But that's impossible. He was right there."

"Eddie suffered a heart attack and died while playing dominoes with us at that very table," said Tony. "That was our spot. We played there Mondays, Wednesdays, and Fridays."

"Eddie was a peach of a friend," added Joe. "Always laughing and smiling. If you needed a favor, he was always glad to do one. If you were short a few bucks, he'd give you some—not loan it, but give it to you. Unfortunately, he was in poor health, and we all knew he didn't have long to live. Still, it was a shock."

Jayne put her hands to her face, trying to recover from the stunning news. "I can't believe what you're telling me. I saw him just a little while ago. I really did."

Joe turned to his friend and whispered, "Tony, you don't suppose that Eddie came back . . . you know . . . hoping to make contact?"

Jayne shivered at the thought. "What are you saying? That I saw his ghost?"

"That would be like Eddie," Joe replied. "He always said he hoped to return from the dead."

"Then how come neither one of you saw him and I did?" asked Jayne.

Tony shook his head. "I don't know. Eddie was an artist who loved to paint. Maybe this was his way of making contact with us—through you. You're an artist . . . and a darn good one, I might add."

Jayne could feel herself shake all over. She leaned against the fence and slowly slid down to the ground. "I'm getting a little scared."

Seeing the frightened look on the young girl's face broke Tony's heart. "We're terribly sorry, Jayne" he said.

"Please forgive us. Joe and I are two old codgers who are probably a little touched in the head. You know, senile. Don't pay us any mind. Just forget everything we've said. I guess we're still hurting from Eddie's death, and we miss him very much."

But as Jayne looked into their sorrowful eyes, she could tell that they truly believed she had seen Eddie—and drawn his ghost.

"Um, what are you going to do with the sketch?" Joe asked her.

"I usually take my drawings home."

"Could we buy it, please? It would mean a lot to us."

Jayne thought a moment and said, "It's not for sale." Then she grinned and handed Joe the drawing. "It's free—a gift from me to you."

* * *

Whenever Jayne felt troubled and wanted to escape, she would get out her tubes of acrylic paint and create on canvas a soothing landscape, usually of spring flowers or autumn leaves. That night, hours after her startling experience at Carlin Park, she set up her easel and canvas in her bedroom. She didn't want to think any more about the ghost. She had told her parents what had happened, but their explanation didn't satisfy her. They figured she had simply drawn someone who had looked like Eddie.

Hoping to forget about her day, Jayne decided to paint a scene of the gardens by the pond at Manville Park. Using a pencil first, she lightly drew an outline of what she wanted to color. Then she went to the brush. But she couldn't concentrate on her painting. She kept reliving her day in the park and seeing Eddie's face in her mind. After about 30 minutes, she gave up and put her paints away because she was simply too emotionally spent. Still in her T-shirt and shorts, she sprawled on her bed and fell fast asleep.

When Jayne woke up the next morning and headed for the bathroom, she happened to glance at her just-started painting. "What's this?" she asked herself out loud. The outline of a young girl sitting among the flowers had been drawn in pencil in the center of the garden.

She immediately assumed that her father, an amateur artist himself, had drawn it. She called him into her room and asked, "Did you draw this last night?"

"No, honey," he replied. "That's not my style. Actually, it looks a lot like yours."

"I didn't draw it, Dad. At least I don't remember doing it. Maybe I'm still shook up from yesterday."

Jayne didn't touch the painting the entire day or that evening either. But she received an emotional jolt the next morning. While she was getting dressed, she accidentally bumped into the canvas, knocking if off the easel. She picked it up and reeled in shock. "I don't believe it!" she cried out. Drawn in pencil were more detailed features of the girl, who looked about four years old with straight hair and bangs and big eyes. She bore a cute smile with a missing front tooth.

"Am I going loony or what?" Jayne wondered out loud. She didn't have the answer, and that scared her. *Why can't I remember drawing this?* She thought long and hard—until she snapped her fingers. *Maybe I did it in my sleep! I'll bet that's it. Why not? If people can sleep-*

walk, I can sleeppaint! But why would this happen to me all of a sudden when I've never sleepwalked before? And why would I draw this particular little girl? I draw only real people, and I've never seen her before. Who could she be?

As the questions swirled around in her brain, she started to get a headache. *Maybe I should just paint over all this and start again. Yes, I think that's what I'll do tonight.*

Late that evening, Jayne was about to cover the sketch with paint when a weird feeling crept over her. Something held her back from covering the drawing of the girl. She began to think that somehow, some way this mysterious work-in-progress would hold great meaning when it was finished. But why it should and for whom, Jayne had no idea.

Now moved by an urge to complete the entire painting, Jayne dabbed the canvas with bright colors for the marigolds, pansies, and other flowers. Eventually, as the clock approached midnight, the only part of the canvas not painted was the pencil sketch of the little girl.

Jayne studied the girl for several minutes. *What color should I make her hair? Her eyes? The tone of her skin? And why do I suddenly feel nervous about this? Why do I have butterflies in my stomach?*

She dipped her brush into the flesh-colored paint and began to spread it on the girl's face. Slowly and carefully, Jayne worked to get the face just right. Even though it was a face she had never seen before, she seemed to know exactly what it should look like. By now, Jayne's legs and back were aching because it was so late. She didn't want to quit, but her eyelids were getting droopy.

* * *

Where am I? What's happened? wondered Jayne as she opened her eyes. The clock by the side of the bed said 3:23. I must have dozed off. She was laying on top of her bedspread and could barely keep her eyes open more than a slit because the bedroom lights were still on.

As she rolled over, Jayne suddenly had an eerie feeling that she wasn't alone in the room. She slowly turned to her right, toward the canvas, and had the shock of her life.

There, standing only a few feet away from her, was Eddie! Or was it his ghost? Wearing the same green golf shirt and red-and-green plaid pants that he had on when she first saw him days earlier, Eddie was busily putting the finishing touches on the little girl in the painting. A brush stroke here, a brush stroke there. Then he stepped back, tweaked his mustache, and eyed the canvas.

Jayne was too awed to move a muscle or say a word. She just watched through half-closed eyes, pretending to be asleep. She wasn't as scared as she thought she'd be with a ghost in her room. He didn't seem like someone—or something—who would harm her. Just the same, her heart pounded furiously and she broke out in a sweat. But she remained still, hoping she wouldn't spook him.

Within a few minutes, Eddie lay down his brush. He stepped back, nodded approvingly, and smiled. Then he put his index and middle fingers together, kissed them, and gently placed them over the lips of the little girl in the drawing.

"Sara," he whispered. And then Eddie vanished.

Jayne stayed frozen for several minutes before she sat up in bed. Trembling, she yelled out, "Daddy! Daddy!"

Her father burst into the room. "What's the matter, honey?"

"He was here! He was here!"

"Who?"

"Eddie, the old man. The ghost. He was here and he finished the painting. Look!"

Her father stared at the painting. Sitting among the flowers was a cute little girl with pale blue eyes, golden hair in a ponytail, and wearing a flowered dress with a white lace collar.

"It's a pretty painting," said her father, "but are you sure a ghost worked on this? You were painting late into the night, right? I bet you finished it and then fell asleep and dreamed about Eddie."

"But he was here! I saw him!" Then she looked in the lower right-hand corner of the painting. Scrawled in black were the initials E.V. "Eddie's last name was Vitale. How do you explain that?"

Her father shrugged. "It's hard for me to believe that Eddie the ghost visited you," he said. "But I can tell that you believe it. Did he say anything to you?"

"No, but I did hear him say the name Sara. That must be the name of the girl in the picture."

"Do you know her?"

"No, but I think I can find out who she is."

The next morning, Jayne took the painting with her to Carlin Park and found Joe and Tony playing dominoes at the same table where she'd last seen them.

"Well, hello, Jayne," beamed Joe. "We wondered if we'd ever see you again."

"Joe, Tony, I have something to show you." She held up the painting of the little girl. "Eddie came to my house and painted her. I saw his ghost last night. When he finished, he called out the name 'Sara' and then he just disappeared."

The two old men whistled in amazement. "Eddie always finished whatever he set out to do," said Joe.

"That's Eddie for you," added Tony. "Jayne, Eddie loved doing portraits, especially of his grandchildren. In fact, just before he died, he told us he was about to paint a picture of his youngest granddaughter. We thought it was a shame that he never had a chance to do it."

"But he found a way to paint her even after he died," Joe declared. "You see, the girl in this painting is his granddaughter. Her name is Sara."

"So what you're saying is that Eddie couldn't leave this world until he finished painting Sara," said Jayne, her eyes wide with amazement. "I hope now he can rest in peace."

THE HOUSE OF MURDER

ifteen-year-old Luis Cardenal was helping his family unload the furniture from the back of their rented truck. Despite the cold, snowy weather, the muscular high school athlete had worked up a sweat from carrying the heaviest boxes. He was taking off his school jacket when a short middle-aged man in a torn blue winter coat stopped him on the sidewalk.

"So you're moving in there, huh?" asked the man, brushing the falling snow from his scraggly brown hair.

"That's right," Luis replied, picking up two kitchen chairs under each arm.

"You do know about this place, don't you?"

"What do you mean?" Luis set the chairs down and stared at the strange man.

"Oh, you'll find out," the man snickered. As he moved on, he shook his head and chuckled the way a child does when he knows something that his friends don't. "You'll find out soon enough."

Luis, his two younger sisters Rosie and Renee, and their mother Elena rented the cramped, ugly, two-story brick house because it was all they could afford after their mom's recent divorce. The house was old and creaky—like so many others on the busy street—with a cranky furnace and rust-stained kitchen appliances. But at least it had a fireplace.

The very first night in the house, Luis found some chopped wood under the crumbling back stoop, lugged it inside, and built a roaring fire in the living room. That's the way Luis was—a take-charge person who didn't have to wait to be told what to do. With the firewood crackling and the flames flickering, the family sat on the bare floor, drinking hot chocolate and talking about their new life.

"I'm sure going to miss the old neighborhood," said Renee, Luis' 13-year-old sister.

"But at least we can stay in the same schools," Luis pointed out. "And I'll be able to stay on the football team."

"I don't know if I like this house," added Rosie, 10, the youngest in the Cardenal family. "It gives me the creeps. It's old and it smells funny."

"I know it's not the safest area, but it's the best we can do," sighed their mother. "Besides, we're very fortunate to have a house where the rent is so cheap. I can't believe we got such a bargain."

"And I can't believe I could make such an awesome fire," beamed Luis. "First time ever. Pretty neat."

"Yeah, I'm toasty warm," said Rosie.

"Not me," Renee complained. "It sure doesn't seem to be kicking out much heat. I'm cold. There's an awful chill in the room."

"You've got to be kidding," said Luis. "It's almost too warm in here."

"Come over here," she said. "You'll see for yourself." Luis scooted over to Renee, who was sitting just three feet away from the flames on the far left side of the fireplace. Luis instantly felt a coldness.

"That's weird," he said. "It feels like the air when you open up a refrigerator door." He stood up and, after taking a few steps, discovered that the cold spot was the size of a throw rug, roughly three feet by three feet. Luis straddled an edge of the cold spot. Then, by spreading his arms straight out, he noticed his right hand felt warm from the fire while his left hand, which was inside the chilly area, was cold.

Luis kneeled down and put his hands a few inches above the floor, trying to feel for any draft that might be coming from under the house through the cracks of the wood planks. "There's no draft or anything," he reported. "Just cold."

He stared at the dark wood for a moment and said, "Hey, look at this." He pointed to a barely visible but large oval-shaped stain on the floor. "It seems to match the cold spot. I wonder what it is."

The startling answer would come soon enough.

That night the Cardinals had just gone to bed when they heard a noise that sent their hair on end—footsteps of someone walking up the stairs. CREAK . . . CREAK . . . CREAK. The footsteps were slow as though the person was trying to be quiet but the squeaky stairs betrayed him.

"Luis? Is that you?" his mother asked from her bedroom.

"No, Mom," he answered from bed.

"Rosie? Renee? Are either one of you on the stairway?"

"No, Mama," Renee replied in a voice wavering with fear. "We're in bed."

Luis knew the telephone hadn't been connected yet, so he couldn't call 911. *I've got to do something—and fast,* he told himself. He quickly slipped out of his bed and grabbed a baseball bat from the closet. His bedroom was nearest the stairs, so he stood by the open doorway and waited. CREAK . . . CREAK . . . CREAK. The footsteps were coming closer and closer, and then they stopped.

Luis assumed the intruder had reached the top of the landing—only a few feet away from him. Luis' hands started to sweat as he gripped the bat tighter. *Another few steps and I'll clobber him!* He held his breath, listening for any sound like breathing or more footsteps. But all he heard was the sound of his own heart pounding furiously.

For what seemed like an eternity—but was actually only a minute—the hallway remained silent. Finally, Luis could stand it no more. *One . . . two . . . three. Here I go!* He leaped out into the black hallway, gave his best imitation of a ninja battle cry, and swung his bat wildly from side to side.

"Rosie! Renee! Stay put!" shouted Elena. She dashed

out into the hall and flicked on the light switch. But there was no one there except Luis, still swinging his bat in the air.

"Where did he go?" he asked, half in relief that he hadn't faced an intruder and half in bewilderment for the same reason. Together, Luis and his mother cautiously walked down the stairs and checked the living room, dining room, and kitchen. The windows were still locked and the doors were still bolted, including the one to the basement.

"It's probably like that cold spot—just another one of the quirks of this house," Elena said with a nervous laugh.

"Let's hope there aren't any more," Luis added.

He and his mother walked into the girls' room and found them cowering under their covers. "It's all right, girls," said Elena soothingly. "It was nothing—just one of the ways the house 'talks' to us."

"Well, I hope it shuts up from now on," said Rosie.

Luis returned to his bedroom, but he couldn't go back to sleep. *Somebody was climbing those stairs,* he told himself. *The steps don't creak like that on their own. Somebody was here. But if that's true, where is he? Who is he? I'd better keep this bat in bed with me.*

* * *

The next day, Luis was carrying out empty boxes and placing them at the curb for the trash pickup when the weird man approached him for the second time. Luis had already taken a dislike to him.

"Did you and your family sleep well your first night in the house?" the man asked.

"Why wouldn't we?" said Luis.

"Oh, no reason. See you around."

"Hey, wait a minute," said Luis. "We thought we heard someone in our house last night. You wouldn't know anything about that, would you?"

The man vigorously shook his head. "Oh, heavens no. I wouldn't be caught dead in that house—unlike some other people." He gave a little laugh. "Now, if you'll excuse me, I'll be on my way."

The Cardenals continued to unpack their things and get settled in their new surroundings. By bedtime, they were exhausted, but they still found it hard to go to sleep. They were worried they would hear those frightening footsteps again. This time, they left the light on in the hallway and closed their bedroom doors.

When Luis woke up very early the next morning, he breathed a sigh of relief. Nothing unusual had happened during the night. Or so he thought. It was still dark as he opened his bedroom door and shuffled toward the bathroom. *That's funny,* he thought. *I know Mom left the hall light on when we went to bed last night, but it's not on now.*

At the breakfast table, Rosie tugged at her mother's sleeve. "Mama, are you all right?"

Elena cocked her head, surprised by the question. "I'm fine, Rosie. Why do you ask?"

"Well, um, I heard you crying last night."

Elena bent over so she was eye-level with her daughter. "Honey, I wasn't crying."

"We heard you, Mama, right after we all went to bed," said Renee.

"Girls, I can assure you it wasn't me. Just what did you hear?"

"A woman was crying," said Rosie.

"More like a whimper," Renee added. "Actually it sounded like it was coming from our room, but it couldn't have been. So we figured it had to be you. The crying lasted about ten minutes."

The girls and their mother turned to Luis. "Hey, it wasn't me," he said. "Besides, I didn't hear anything. By the way, who turned off the hall light last night?"

Everyone at the table shook their head. "Well, it was off when I got up this morning."

"This house is giving me goose bumps," Rosie complained.

"Oh, it's nothing but the strangeness of the new surroundings, that's all," explained their mother, not very convincingly. She rubbed her fingers through her hair as she searched for a way to stop this scary talk. "Kids, look, this is our home now. We have to get used to it. I don't want to hear any more talk about footsteps and crying women."

Later that afternoon, while their mother was still at work, the three kids came home from school together. When they opened the front door, they were stunned by a high-pitched scream: "Nooooooo!"

"It's coming from upstairs!" shouted Luis. "Stay here. If I'm not back in one minute, go next door and call for help." He bounded up the steps and then warily peeked into his room. Nothing. He looked in his mother's room. Still nothing. But then he heard a woman sob at the end of the hall from behind the girls' closed bedroom door.

Luis tiptoed up to the door and then flung it open. The crying stopped instantly. He looked throughout the room and found no one, but his eye caught something on the floor. It was a butcher knife. "What the . . ."

"Luis, are you all right?" Renee shouted.

"Yes, I'm fine." He walked back down the stairs with the knife and asked, "We all heard that scream, right?" The girls nodded. "And it was coming from upstairs, right?" Again they nodded. "I heard crying coming from your room, yet no one was there. But look what I found by your bed."

"That's Mama's butcher knife," said Renee. "What was it doing up there?"

"That's what I'd like to know." Luis turned to Rosie. "Did you take that knife upstairs?"

"No way," she said crossing her heart. "Luis, I'm scared."

"I don't blame you, Rosie. Something is going on here, and I sure wish I knew what it is. Meanwhile, let's not tell Mama about this—at least not now. She's going through a rough time with the divorce and the move and all that. She'll freak out for sure."

* * *

When the kids stepped off the school bus the next afternoon, they wondered what they would see or hear when they opened their front door. But before they reached the house, Luis spotted the strange man across the street. "Renee, Rosie, you stay here," said Luis. "I'll be right back. I want to talk to this guy first."

As Luis approached him, the man said, "Hello, again. So how do you like living there?"

"You seem awfully interested in us and our house," said Luis.

"Just trying to be neighborly, that's all."

Luis, who stood several inches taller and was about 50 pounds heavier than the man, leaned into his face and said, "I've got to be honest with you. You're bugging me. You keep asking me strange questions. Now I've got one for you. What's going on in our house?"

"I don't know what you're talking about," said the man.

"I think you do." Throwing a muscular arm around the man's shoulder so he couldn't get away, Luis said, "Let's go inside and warm up, and you can tell me all about it."

The man froze. His eyes turned wild. "No! No! I can't go in there!" He broke free from Luis' grasp and tried to run away.

"Hey, wait a second!" shouted Luis. "What's going on? Why are you so afraid to come into our house?" Luis quickly caught up with him and blocked his path. "Listen, mister. My family is scared to death because of things we've heard. Whatever you know about this place, you've got to tell me. Please."

"Okay, okay," said the man. "But I'm not going inside." He sat down on the street curb and motioned for Luis to do the same. "You're not going to like what I'm about to tell you. Back about ten years ago, an ex-convict by the name of Fenton Morris lived there. He was bad news. Spent time in prison for armed robbery and assault. Rotten to the core.

"One night he and his girlfriend Charlotte Webster, a

waitress at the coffee shop down the street, got into a big fight upstairs in the house. He dragged her downstairs, and she was screaming. It just so happened that I was walking by at the time, so I peaked into the window. She was struggling and then . . ." He lowered his eyes and shook his head. "He stabbed her with a butcher knife. There was nothing I could do to stop it. I'm just a little guy. So I ran next door and had the neighbors call the police. The police found her body in a big pool of blood by the fireplace."

"The left side of the fireplace?"

"Yeah, I think so."

"The cold spot!" said Luis, snapping his fingers.

"The what?"

"Never mind. Go on."

"Well, the police arrested Morris," the man said. "He was found guilty of murder and ended up dying in the electric chair. Ever since then, people who have rented the house have been spooked by Charlotte's crying ghost and have faced the wrath of Fenton Morris' ghost. No one has been able to live there more than a month without fleeing in terror."

Luis stared long and hard at the man, wondering whether or not to believe him. "No ghosts are going to run me and my family out of this house!" declared Luis. "That's assuming there are ghosts inside."

"Don't assume it, young man. Believe it."

The frightening incidents over the past few days certainly seemed to back up the man's story. The more he thought about it, the more scared and angry Luis became. So he decided to take matters into his own hands.

Returning to his sisters, Luis unlocked the front door and stepped inside, waiting and wondering what would happen next. But the house seemed quiet and peaceful. "Everything is fine, girls," he announced. "Mom left us some money to buy a few things for tonight's dinner. Here's the list. Would you please walk to the store and get them?"

"Why don't you do it?" asked Renee.

"I'll start us a fire in the fireplace and make some hot chocolate . . . and I'll let you keep all the change."

"All right!" said Rosie.

After the girls left, Luis went upstairs and into their bedroom. He felt somewhat silly about what he was going to do next, but he figured he'd give it a try. Walking around the room, he announced in a firm clear voice, "Okay, Charlotte, you're dead! You're a ghost. And you don't belong here. I don't think you mean to, but you're scaring my family. So I want you out of here right now. You're supposed to go where all the other spirits go, wherever that is. Now leave us alone!"

Then Luis stormed downstairs and stood directly in the cold spot. He shivered a couple of times not only from the chill but from knowing a woman was killed on that very spot—that the stain on the floor was from Charlotte's blood.

"As for you, Fenton Morris, you might have scared other people out of here, but not me. You're dead—you fried in the electric chair. I don't care how evil you are, this house is full of love, so there's no room for a ghost like you. You don't belong here. You're not wanted here. Now clear out and stay out! And if you think you're so powerful, then let's see you try something right now."

With fists clenched by his side and his nerves on edge, Luis paced back and forth in the living room, waiting for something terrible to happen—and hoping nothing would. Sweat beaded on his forehead, and his breathing turned shallow. At any moment, the ghost could attack him. And then . . .

The front door swung open, and Luis jumped with fright. "We're baa-aack!" shouted Rosie.

That night at the dinner table, Luis confidently declared, "I don't think we're going to have any more strange things happening around here. It's like Mom said. We have to get used to our new surroundings. This is an old house so there are bound to be creaks and noises and things."

Nothing out of the ordinary occurred over the next few days and nights, which convinced Luis that he finally had rid the house of the ghosts. But he was wrong. Very wrong.

A week after the Cardenals had moved in, Luis was awakened in the middle of the night by the sensation of someone pounding once on his pillow. He raised his head and, with the help of the hall light shining through his open bedroom door, looked around the room. Then he lay down again, rolled over on his other side . . . and felt something cold and hard against his nose. He opened his eyes and screamed, "AAAAAHHH!" Luis bolted out of bed and flicked on the light. Someone had plunged his mother's butcher knife through Luis' pillow—inches from his head—and into the mattress.

Across the hall, Elena Cardenal, hearing her son's

terrified shout, sprang out of bed. But some unexplainable force, like an invisible pair of hands, shoved her back down. She managed to turn on the bedside light and saw to her horror a glass bottle of hand lotion rise up about six inches and then crash on top of her bedside table. As the lotion spread out over the tabletop, an invisible finger spelled out "LEAVE" in the lotion.

Meanwhile in the girls' room, the eerie wailing and sobbing of an unseen woman jarred Renee and Rosie out of their sleep. Screaming with fright, they dashed out of their room and into the hallway. Elena, finally free from the clutches of the invisible force, ran out of her room as did Luis. The Cardenals scrambled down the stairs, turned on the lights, and huddled in the middle of the living room. They held each other tight and no one said a word. Only their whimpers and gasps echoed off the bare walls.

"Oh, no, look!" shouted Luis, pointing to the cold spot by the fireplace. A smoky cloud about six feet high suddenly appeared and slowly began to swirl from the top down into the shape of a person. The Cardenals were so petrified that their feet seemed glued to the floor. With disbelieving eyes, they watched a head form, then eyes, nose, and a mouth. As the details of the face came into view, Rosie let out a wail and buried her head in her mother's stomach.

In the cold spot stood a menacing man reeking with evil. A thick ugly scar ran from his arched right eyebrow across the top of his bald head. His green eyes burned with hate, and his mouth twisted into a heart-stopping sneer. Gray stubble lined his bony cheeks and chin. And in his right hand he clutched a butcher knife—a long curved blade dripping with blood.

"Run, kids, run!" shouted Elena. Screaming in terror, they dashed next door to their landlords, the Colemans.

When Mrs. Coleman opened her door and took one look into the eyes of the horror-struck family, she cried with alarm, "Oh, no, not again!"

Once she calmed them down, Mrs. Coleman confessed that the Cardenals were the sixth tenants to flee in the middle of the night—scared out of their wits by ghosts.

"Promise me you will never rent that house again," said Elena, still shaking from the ordeal.

"I promise," said Mrs. Coleman. The Cardenals found a new place to live, but their old rented house has remained empty—empty except for maybe the tormented ghosts of Charlotte Webster and Fenton Morris.

THE PHANTOM PRANKSTER

**A**ndy Jordan loved to pull pranks on his family. But during one unforgettable weekend, he became the target of a barrage of practical jokes from a prankster whose identity sent chills down his spine.

Eleven-year-old Andy, his fourteen-year-old brother Steve, and fifteen-year-old sister Suzanne, lived with their parents out in the country in a two-story wood-frame house with a wrap-around porch. Life was pleasant and uneventful in the Jordan home—except when Andy displayed his devilish sense of humor.

He was always leaving silly phone messages for his father. It was usually something like: "Dad, call Mr. Beagle. Here's his number." When Mr. Jordan dialed the number and asked for Mr. Beagle, he sheepishly learned that he had called the animal shelter. About once a month, Andy would place a fake beetle or spider in a kitchen cabinet and wait for his mother to scream.

Andy aimed his best pranks at his brother and sister. Once, while Steve was taking a shower, Andy sneaked into the bathroom and sprayed his brother's white towel with whipped cream. When Steve came out of the shower to dry off, he didn't realize until it was too late that he had spread whipped cream all over his face. Another time, Andy secretly poured talcum powder in Suzanne's hair dryer. When she flipped it on, her head became covered with powder.

His victims sought revenge with practical jokes of their own, but Andy usually caught on in the nick of time to spoil the fun—that is, until the day he met his match.

* * *

One Saturday morning, while Andy was carrying a basket of clean laundry upstairs, he tripped on a loose step. When he examined the step, he discovered that the wood top—the part you walk on—had become very loose. After removing the board, he looked inside and found to his surprise a slingshot made out of a sturdy tree branch, a leather bag full of marbles, an old Batman comic book, a red rubber ball, a Slinky, a three-inch-tall World War II tin soldier, and a palm-sized plastic submarine—a cereal box prize—with instructions on how to propel it in the water with an aspirin.

He also found a yellowed fifth-grade report card belonging to Peter Worthy and dated June 15, 1957. For the semester, Peter earned C's in reading, arithmetic, and science, and B's in penmanship, physical fitness, and geography. In a section for comments, the teacher had written, "Has the brains to be the class leader but chooses to be the class clown." The report card came from Shirland Township Elementary School—the same one that Andy now attended.

"Hey, Mom! Come here and see what I found!" Andy shouted.

After closely examining the items, she said, "This must have been Peter Worthy's secret hiding place."

"Who is Peter Worthy?"

"He's probably related to Homer and Cecilia Worthy. They're the ones who sold the house to us ten years ago. I remember meeting their three grown daughters, but the Worthys never mentioned a son."

Andy took Peter's things out of the hiding spot and put them on his desk. A short while later, the rest of the family went into town to shop. Andy stayed home where he played with the old Slinky and watched a *Brady Bunch* rerun on TV. But just when he was enjoying the show, the TV set went off. At first Andy thought the power had gone out. But he noticed that the lights were still on in the room, so he walked over to the set and fiddled with the knob.

That's funny, he thought. *It turned off by itself.* He pushed the on-off button, and the TV sprang back to life. Then he returned to his chair to watch the show. But a couple of minutes later, the TV set went off again. *What's going on here?* He turned the TV back on. A minute later, it clicked off for the third time. *That's it,* he told himself. *I give up. This dumb old set, I hate it. We've got to get a new one—and it had better have a remote control.*

As Andy left the living room, he heard an eerie sing-song laugh that lasted a few seconds: "Ha, ha, ha . . . ha, ha, ha." Andy had never heard such a laugh and had no idea who it was—although it sounded like a boy—or where the laugh had come from. Andy peered out the window but didn't see anyone. Not giving it another thought, he went upstairs to his bedroom, picked up the old Batman comic book he had found in Peter's stash, and plopped on his bed.

The pages had turned brown and brittle from age, so he handled the comic book carefully as he read about the Caped Crusader's adventure. But then his bedside light flicked off by itself. He turned it back on. Seconds later, it turned off again. He slammed the comic book down in disgust and thought, *What's going on here? Why is everything electrical that I touch acting bonkers? I'm going outside.*

The frustrated boy grabbed the comic book and the slingshot he had found the day before. As he went out the front door, he tossed the comic book on the porch rocking chair and walked to the gravel driveway. There, he picked up stones and fired them one at a time from the slingshot, hitting the trunk of a nearby elm tree.

As Andy turned to walk back into the house, he heard a bang and saw that the front door had closed. He tried the knob but it wouldn't turn. *Oh no! It's locked!* He ran around to the back only to find that the kitchen door was also latched. He checked all the windows but they were closed tight except for the one in his bedroom upstairs.

It was beginning to drizzle so Andy decided to enter the house through that open window. He climbed up a trellis—a frame of long wooden strips attached to the side of the house on which thick ivy was growing. At the top, he crawled onto the roof of the porch. Just as he was about to reach the window, it slammed shut by itself with a loud thud. He tried opening it, but no matter how hard he struggled, the window wouldn't budge. "Oh, man! Are you kidding me?" Andy shouted out loud. "I don't believe this!"

By now, the drizzle had turned into a steady rain. Fuming mad, Andy climbed back down the ivy, slipping the final five feet and falling splat into a mud puddle.

Again, he heard that same kid's sing-song laughter: "Ha, ha, ha . . . ha, ha, ha."

Wet, dirty, and angry, Andy stormed back to the porch. *Well, at least I can read Batman,* he thought. But when he looked at the rocker, the comic book was gone. *I did leave it there, didn't I? I'm sure I did. Where could it be?* He searched every inch of the porch but couldn't find it. *I bet that kid I heard laughing swiped it. I wonder who he is. Boy, if I catch him . . .* With nothing to do but watch the rain, Andy sat glumly in the rocker and waited for nearly two hours before his family arrived. When they heard about his troubling day, they enjoyed a hearty chuckle at his expense.

"Andy, I thought you said you didn't have anything to read," said his father.

"I didn't."

"What's this?" His father held up the old Batman comic book.

"Where did you find that?" asked Andy, totally stunned.

"Sitting right here on the chair."

"But, but that's impossible. I've been sitting there for the last couple of hours and it wasn't there."

"Maybe you need glasses," Steve piped in.

Andy walked into the house in a daze, wondering if his brain had short-circuited.

* * *

Thump! Thump! Thump!

Andy was stirred out of his sleep by the sound of a ball bouncing on the floor of his room. He groped for the light, but as soon as he turned it on, the noise stopped. *I must have been dreaming,* he thought. He turned off the light and started to go back to sleep when . . .

Thump! Thump! Thump!

"Andy! What's all that racket in your room?" shouted his father from across the hall.

"I don't know, Dad." Like before, the noise stopped the moment Andy turned on the light. He looked around the room and spotted Peter's red rubber ball resting motionless in the middle of the floor. Before he had gone to sleep that night, Andy had been tossing it in the air and catching it behind his back. Then he had set it on his desk and gone to bed. "It's a rubber ball, Dad. It must have fallen off my desk." But Andy had no explanation for why the ball had stopped bouncing and then started up again.

The next morning, Andy took the tiny plastic submarine into the bathroom where he inserted an aspirin into the back of the sub and placed it in a sink full of water.

The sub, powered by a chemical reaction between the aspirin and the water, scooted back and forth across the sink.

Bored after a couple of minutes, Andy hopped into the shower. He had just lathered up his face with soap when the hot water suddenly turned icy cold. The freezing shock nearly took his breath away. His hands quickly reached the temperature handle, which was now on the coldest setting, and tried turning it, but it wouldn't move.

Andy couldn't stand the cold any longer. With his eyes still closed to keep out the soap, he stumbled out of the shower, fumbling for a towel. But it wasn't on the towel rack where he had left it. The soaking wet boy blindly hunted for something, anything, to wipe the soap from his face. He banged his shin against the toilet and stubbed his toe on the sink pedestal. By chance, he stepped on his towel, which apparently had fallen. Andy picked it up and dried his face.

He immediately thought that Steve had pulled a dirty trick on him. But the door to the bathroom was still locked from the inside, so he knew his brother couldn't have done it. By now, Andy was totally befuddled, especially when he noticed that the shower now was spewing hot water. He reached in to shut off the water and this time the handle moved with ease.

As he wondered what confounding thing would happen to him next, Andy turned on the sink water to brush his teeth. He unscrewed the cap to the toothpaste and squeezed the tube, but nothing came out even though it was full. Andy looked down at the opening and squeezed harder. *This doesn't make sense,* he thought. *Why would it . . . ahhhhh!* Suddenly, half the toothpaste squirted out in a foot-long stream that plastered Andy's face, sticking to his nose and eyelids.

He cleaned the toothpaste off his face and stared into the steamy mirror above the sink—and his jaw dropped from amazement. The words "HA HA" had formed on the glass.

Before Andy could react, a loud pounding noise echoed in the room, causing him to jump a foot off the floor. "Hey, hurry up in there!" yelled Steve. "I gotta go."

Andy unlocked the door and turned the knob, but it wouldn't open. "It's stuck!" he declared.

"Quit joking around! I really have to go!"

"Push on your side and I'll yank from my side," said Andy. He tugged and pulled. Then, just as Steve charged the door with his shoulder, it whipped open and he flew halfway across the bathroom, landing in a heap.

"You did that on purpose, didn't you?" said Steve. "Another one of your little jokes."

"It was stuck, really it was," replied Andy.

"I'll get even with you for this."

"You didn't happen to write something on the bathroom mirror before I went in there, did you?"

"No, but if I had thought about it, I'd have written 'JERK' in big letters."

Later that morning, Andy took the tin soldier he'd found in the hiding place and put it in the seat of his remote-control drag racer. He expertly maneuvered it through the legs of the dining room table and around the living room couch. But his fun was interrupted when his mother announced, "Would everyone come into the den, please. And, Andy, turn off that drag racer."

When the family was assembled, she told them, "I just got off the phone with Mrs. Worthy, the dear lady who used to live here. I told her about finding those toys and things in the step and asked her if she knew who Peter Worthy was. It turns out that Peter was her son. Then she told me something very sad. Peter died when he was only ten years old—in the summer of 1957."

"Then that must mean I've got his very last report card," said Andy. "How did he die?"

"It seems he was a real prankster. Does that remind you of anyone in our family? Well, one day he filled a balloon full of water and was stringing it high in a tree. He was rigging it so that with one pull of the string from the ground, the water balloon would fall on the head of one of his sisters as she walked by. But he fell out of the tree, broke his neck, and died."

"Oh, how awful!" said Suzanne.

"What about the things we found in the step?" asked Andy.

"Mrs. Worthy didn't know about the secret hiding place," said his mother. "She'd love to get all of Peter's things back, so Andy, put them in a box and —"

Suddenly, Andy's drag racer roared off and began banging into the furniture.

"Andy!" his mother said sternly. "I thought I told you to turn that off!"

Andy fiddled with the remote control. "I've lost control!" he shouted. "It's going crazy all by itself!" The drag racer smashed into his mother's bare feet, made a right turn, and crashed into a vase on the floor, shattering it into dozens of pieces.

"Stop it!" his mother demanded. "Turn it off this instant!"

"I'm trying, Mom! But it just keeps going! Look out!"

The drag racer's back air foil caught the hem of one of the handmade, floor-length lace drapes and ripped it off the curtain rod.

"Oh no!" Andy cried. He and Steve chased after it, but the drag racer dodged, twirled, and weaved before Andy captured it with a diving leap. Only after he had ripped out the batteries did the car whine and then die.

"Boy, are you in trouble now!" said Steve with a grin.

"I don't know how that happened," said Andy, shaking his head in bewilderment. "It started up and went out of control like it was doing its own thing."

"Give me that toy!" stormed his father. "You're through playing with this. And you're going to pay for all the damage. I'm going to take it out of your allowance."

"But Dad —"

"No buts, young man. You're responsible for this mess."

From behind them came that strange sing-song laughter: "Ha, ha, ha . . . ha, ha, ha."

"Steven," said his father, "this is not funny."

"Don't blame me," replied Steve. "I wasn't laughing."

"Then who was?"

"Probably Peter Worthy," Andy said sarcastically.

* * *

The more Andy thought about it, the more convinced he became that the weird things that had happened to him over the past two days were pranks engineered by none other than Peter's ghost. They all happened after Andy had found the hiding place—and while he was playing with or using one of Peter's things.

That night, as Andy lay in bed, he felt a little nervous thinking that a ghost might be toying with him. Andy wrestled with the idea of confronting the spirit. *Do I really want to see this ghost?* he wondered. *What would I do if he appeared? Dive under the covers? Scream for help? Talk to him? Sounds kind of scary, but here goes.*

From his bed, Andy whispered out loud, "Peter, if you're out there, would you please leave me alone? I don't find your pranks very funny. Your last joke got me into a whole lot of trouble."

Andy lay very still. He wanted a sign that Peter's ghost existed, yet he wouldn't mind if none appeared. All remained silent for a long time until he heard something rolling across the wood floor. Andy could feel his skin crawl and his chest muscles tighten from fear. He turned his head and scanned an area of the floor lit by the moonbeam coming through his window. Out of the shadows rolled one of Peter's marbles—a large green cat's eye. The marble moved, as if by magic, slowly and steadily from one end of the room to the other.

Andy, awed and scared at the same time, slipped out of bed and picked up the marble. *This must be a sign from Peter's ghost,* he thought. Andy rolled it back to the corner where it came from. A nerve-wracking minute later, the marble rolled back toward Andy, coming to rest at his feet.

Andy fought within himself. *Run now! Quick! Get out! No, stay. It's okay. The ghost won't hurt you. He's just playing with me. But I don't like it. I don't want him here anymore.*

Andy nervously cleared his throat and said to the darkness, "Look, ah, I really don't want to see you or anything. Just leave me alone, okay? I won't touch your stuff anymore. We're giving it to your mom, so you don't have to bother me. I know you were just joking around. But it's not funny. So would you please stop?"

Andy rolled the marble back across the floor. Then he waited. But it never returned. Convinced that Peter's ghost had left, a much-relieved Andy climbed into bed. As he lay there, he realized that the ghost had given him a taste of his own medicine.

The next day, Andy's mother returned Peter's things to Mrs. Worthy. From then on Andy was no longer the target of any more strange pranks. Of course, that didn't count the time when Steve secretly rigged a bucket of water over the back door and tricked Andy into stepping outside—where he promptly got drenched!